*Only When I Laugh*

Gladys Workman

Only When I Laugh

PRENTICE-HALL, INC.
Englewood Cliffs, N. J.

To Mamma

who made gallons of coffee and tons of biscuits
for our many friends

Contents

Contents

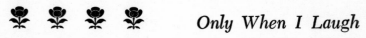

Only When I Laugh

❧ ❧ 1 ❧ ❧

Oh, Dem Golden
Slippers

SOMEONE ONCE REMARKED that I was born with a silver foot in my mouth; meaning, of course, that whenever I stumble—a thing of frequent occurrence—I usually find a featherbed to fall on. There may be some truth in the remark, because all that is wonderful in my life today is the result of a stumbling decision to find health for my sick husband in the Oregon woods.

My husband's illness was not a sudden thing; it showed itself first in extreme listlessness, fatigue and unusual silence. If he spoke at all, it was only to complain of things around the house or at the dye plant he managed. Finally, one Christmas, in our Rosemead, California, home, he collapsed.

The doctor told us it was a puzzling case and it was possible that my husband's blood had been poisoned by the dye chemicals at his plant. But he also warned us that it might be leukemia; at that point he could not be sure. If it was leukemia, the doctor told me, my husband might not have more than six months to live.

It turned out that my husband did not have leukemia, but it was many months before we knew the truth, and I can still feel the way my heart froze at the sound of the doctor's words. Quiet, steady, comforting Pappy had been at my side for over thirty years. *I* had always been the sickly one needing care and comfort. It was unthinkable that anything could happen to Pappy; he was the rock on which I built. But there he was, pale and weak, listless and pathetic, with no real interest in anything going on around him.

There was nothing we could do then, said the doctor, except help Pappy to get some rest. When Pappy agreed to take some time off from the plant and go away, I decided that I wanted to get him out of the city, out where there were green things growing, where the wind was clean, and where he could do some hunting and fishing.

Finding such a place was no problem. I had lived a good many years of my childhood in the beautiful Umpqua Valley of Oregon, and the valley had always remained in my mind as an enchanted land set apart from the world. Through the valley flowed the Umpqua River, and it was on the banks of this river that Pappy and I now decided to spend a week or so.

In Yoncalla, Oregon, which lies just east of the Umpqua Valley, we stayed for a few days at the home of some old friends, the Kruses, to let Pappy rest up from the nine-hundred-mile car trip. The Kruse farm, in earlier days, had been almost like a second home to me.

Our camping-out destination was a point on the Umpqua River near Scottsburg, which stood at the head of tidewater, about twenty miles from the Pacific. During the days we spent there I was delighted to see the way Pappy's eyes lit up as he watched muskrat and otter make long V-wakes in the placid water, or looked up suddenly to see deer scampering daintily into hiding among the myrtlewood trees. He seemed better than he had been for months.

That visit, of necessity, was a short one, but even before we left to return to California, a plan had begun to form in my mind. Somehow I felt that we should come to the Umpqua to live, permanently. If Pappy did have leukemia and there was nothing that could be done for him, at least he could live out his life in surroundings he liked best; if it were found that he only had dye poisoning, which could be cured, life along the Umpqua would be one long step toward the cure. At first, I kept the idea to myself.

Once back in California, however, the idea became hazy; there seemed to be too much standing in the way of it. Pappy had been at the dye plant for twenty-five years; it would not be easy for him to leave. Then there was Young Norman to consider. This was Norman Jackson, our nephew, who had come to stay with us many years before, and was still with us, very much like a son. He was twenty-nine years old, had a good job in a shipyard and might find the idea of leaving it to run off to a remote corner of far western Oregon slightly ridiculous. Then, too, I had my own thriving business as a commercial party hostess. I did not forget the Umpqua, but it began to occupy less and less space in my hopes.

13

Then, one day we had a visitor from Yoncalla, and my dream of Oregon flashed into full-blown life again.

"I've just come down from Yoncalla," said Claude Sherman, a broad-shouldered handsome fellow and a neighbor of the Kruses, when I greeted him at the front door. "Mom Kruse asked me to drop off some squash and chickens she wanted you to have." He said it as matter-of-factly as if he'd just stepped across the street.

We were doing some work on our house at that time and Claude Sherman is, among a great many other things, a masterful carpenter. He came in for a cup of coffee, "just for a minute"; he saw the work we were doing, had another cup, looked around, had another cup, and ended up staying for weeks. The fact that he had only one leg and used crutches didn't prevent him from doing a big portion of the work.

But his presence was even more important than the work that he did, for he was a constant reminder of the streams and forests of Oregon. He talked hunting and fishing to Pappy for hours on end, and Pappy came wonderfully alive when he heard Claude's stories of the big fish he'd caught and the rugged trails he'd combed for deer.

One night, soon after Claude had left, I felt I couldn't hold back the idea any longer and I approached Young Norman. I didn't know how to begin so I just blurted, "You know, this kind of life we're leading isn't getting us anywhere."

"What do you mean?" he asked. "I think we're doing pretty well."

"Oh, sure," I pressed, "but look at Pappy. He doesn't

14

seem to be getting any better, and maybe he's getting worse. You know there's nothing he likes better than hunting and fishing. . . . Let's go up to the Umpqua for good and let him fish and hunt to his heart's content!" I finished in a rush and waited expectantly.

Norman didn't seem too surprised. He thought for a minute and then said, "It's fine with me"—just like that! "I'd like to see that country myself, and I ought to be able to get a job up there just as well as I can down here." There *was* a slight look of doubt on his face, but he didn't say any more.

Pappy didn't need much convincing. When he saw that Norman and I were ready to go, he gave in. We decided we'd like to live as near to Scottsburg as possible, and just the thought of it made Pappy look a little healthier.

Others were not so easily persuaded that moving to the Umpqua made sense. "It's just another of your goofy ideas," said Stella Hardy, a life-long friend. "You're city people and you don't belong in the wilds." I shrugged my shoulders.

"Besides, you're no spring chicken either," she persisted. "You're forty-six and Pappy's over fifty. He'll be needing doctors and you sure won't find them behind the pine trees along that river you're always talking about. And where, may I ask, are you going to stay?"

"When Pappy and I were up there we saw an old cabin on some land by the river that belongs to the Kruses," I said off-handedly. "We could stay there." I didn't want to go too deeply into the problems that faced us; not, at least, until we got to the Umpqua and couldn't turn back. And the objections, somehow, only made me more certain that the Umpqua was the place for Pappy.

We wrote to the Kruses in Yoncalla telling them what we were going to do, and saying we'd like to stay with them for the first few days. Then, in no time at all, it seemed, our house was sold, the cars packed, and we were on our way north.

In Yoncalla we left the highway, turned into a narrow valley, bounced over an old rutted road, passed through an ancient covered bridge, chugged up a long slope through a thirty-acre field and finally arrived at an unpainted, two-story house where the Kruses lived.

There was big, boisterous Dad Kruse to greet us. Looking straight at me he boomed, "Am I going to have to put up with this goddamned nitwit the rest of my life?" All two-hundred pounds of him radiated warmth and affection. I assured him that this goddamned nitwit would be with him only until we could get settled beside the Umpqua. Then, before he could launch his arguments about how foolish we were to think of setting up in the woods, we went to bed.

Before I was completely asleep, it seemed, morning came and I rolled awake. Bright sunlight streamed across the bedroom floor and crawled up the patchwork quilt that covered me. From below came the clicking of Mom Kruse's heels on the kitchen floor as she got breakfast ready.

How many times in the past had I awakened to that rapid, decisive sound! I could almost see Mom, her brown,

16

straight hair drawn back in a bun, her strong, no-nonsense mouth tightly shut as she hurled her ninety pounds of energy at the tasks of the day. Heaven help anyone who got in the way!

I went downstairs and into the kitchen; it was like stepping backward forty years. I could hear the spine-chilling squeak of the old hand-pump, its cough and the final belch which produced a stream of cold, clear water. In the background, the big coffee-grinder rumbled. The room was heavy with the odor of freshly cooked bran muffins and pies (Mom customarily made ten or twelve pies every day, as well as baking bread and the bran muffins that were always on the table).

Mom Kruse looked up and greeted me, her face displaying its usual grimness. Mom has always been rather grim because she feels, and I suppose always will, that the farm will fall apart if she ever loosens her tight hold on the reins. I glanced around the warm kitchen, noticing especially that the woodbox needed filling. To my own hard-won knowledge, that box is impossible to fill; it was my job when I was a girl and I was never able to keep up with the fiery maw of the big woodstove. We sat down in the strands of bright sunlight that cut across the top of the oak table; flies and yellow jackets hummed around the food just as they always had.

I almost felt, sitting at breakfast that first morning with the Kruses, as if I had never been away from Oregon. In the warmth of the kitchen, listening to the Kruses and their sons, Fred and Elmer, it seemed to me for a dreamy moment as if I'd never lived anywhere but in Oregon. And I remember thinking with a smile that my family might not have gone to California and I might have grown up right there in the beautiful North, if President McKinley had not been assassinated.

We lived in Golden Dale, Washington, then, where my father ran the newspaper. He was a good newspaperman, but he had the unshakable notion that if McKinley were left to run loose he would wreck the country. One day my father printed an editorial damning McKinley and his whole administration in terms that were anything but vague. The paper had not been out for half an hour before word came that an assassin had shot the President. By nightfall a McKinley mob had gathered in front of our house, noisy and resenting the ill-timed editorial. My father stood in the living room, shouting to no one in particular that that damned McKinley was a trouble-maker, dead or alive. Hours later, under a full moon, and after most of the mob had gone home to bed, a creaky old wagon headed south from Golden Dale. Beneath a pile of sacks reposed Father, his mind full of curses against the administration that had destroyed the freedom of the press. "They wanted to string me up!" Father would roar whenever he told the story later. "No doubt about it! That's the way McKinley did things!" I think I was fourteen before I realized that that damned McKinley had not personally ordered the mob to converge on our house.

The President's assassination was the shock that eventually shook us loose from the North. After Golden Dale we stayed for a while in Cottage Grove where my father continued his newspapering. For some reason, my only memories of that place concern my personal appearance.

Cottage Grove was a profusion of mountains, Douglas

firs, blackberry vines, roaring streams, and, most interesting to me, large and graceful ferns. I was enamored of
the delicate plants that grew taller than my head. I could
make whole playhouses in them, and even pin them on my
dress to make the most elegant clothes. This was a handy
thing, for my real clothes at that time were somewhat less
imaginative—long-sleeved pinafores with a little Dutch
collar and buttons down the back. I wasn't just dressed, I
was packaged.

Some doctor in Cottage Grove had told my mother to
keep my hair pulled back tight, and she did. This was
supposed to help my eyesight but the hair was skinned
back so tight it pulled my eyes into little slits and I could
hardly see, even with my two pairs of special glasses. I
always dreamed of having wonderful loose, flowing hair
instead of the straight-back stuff that was clamped to my
head.

How long after it was that we moved to California I
can't remember, but my memories of the town to which
we moved are vivid, if rather unusual. Coalinga, which
sprawled in a desolate, desert-like part of the San Joaquin
Valley, was jumping. Oil had just been discovered nearby.
Soon after we got there a magnificent fire added to the
excitement. The blaze brought great satisfaction to all
First Methodists in town because twenty-six saloons went
up in flames. Certain other premises were also destroyed.
I kept hearing talk about "the girls" and where they were
going to move, but no one would answer the questions
I asked. Soon, however, a high fence was put up around a
big old house on the edge of town. At night the red lights
along the fence were simply beautiful. My curiosity

grew when I found a hole under the fence, so I sometimes went there after school. I could hear music and watch "the girls" putting make-up on. I had the pleasure one day of meeting a grown-up friend as he was leaving the premises, but he curtly refused my request for a ride back to town. Father found out about my adventuring, however, and told me not to bother "the girls" any more. So my excursions into the world of lights and music were abruptly halted.

I also had another grown-up friend in Coalinga. Downtown one day I saw the most wonderful machine. It turned out to be a peanut wagon with a heater and a little steam whistle, and there was an old man standing beside it. He was *very* old, and he had only one leg; the other was a wooden peg. I said "Hello," but he seemed cross.

"You want to buy peanuts?"

"No," I answered.

"Then get along," he growled. "Go on, go on."

"I don't think you are very nice," I sniffed. "I just wanted to talk to you."

I ran down to Papa's newspaper office and tearfully told him of the peanut man's rebuff. Papa gave me some money and I bought two handkerchiefs for the old man. When I gave them to him he got a funny look on his face and tried to give me some peanuts. "I don't want any peanuts," I insisted. "I gave you those because I thought you'd be my grandfather." The old man blinked a couple of times, then smiled and said, "Sure, I'll be your grandfather."

That evening Papa told me mysteriously, "Gladys, all your life you might try to do something nice, but today you've done one of the nicest things you'll ever be able to do. That old peanut man was cross with you because he didn't know what to say to a little girl. He was surprised you wanted to talk with him. He hasn't any mother or father or any little girl and your present was the first present he's gotten in a long time." I carried the warmth of those words in my heart for months, and I understood them better when I saw the change that came over the old peanut man. His name was W. R. Brown, but that was just a name he made up for himself because he had been a street waif and never knew his parents or where he came from. He visited our house a lot and in later years he would always show up whenever I had a sick spell. Once, he came all the way from New Orleans, just to talk to me while I lay in bed. Then he just disappeared. I always wondered about him—how he didn't know where he came from and how he just vanished away. It scares me sometimes, when I think of it.

My father's next jump was to Willowbrook, California, and, of course, Mama and I jumped right along with him. Willowbrook is memorable for me because it was then that I finally reached the dizzying heights of the third grade in grammar school; we had moved around so much that I had never officially gotten out of the first grade.

But Willowbrook was the scene of even pleasanter triumphs for me. It was there that romance came into my life. One day, while I was in the front yard, the delivery boy, Dick Smith, drove up in an old Florence Trading Company wagon. He had a friend with him, Norman Workman, fresh from Kentucky, whom he was taking around for introductions. Norman was very quiet, had the deepest, softest brown eyes and a great shock of brown hair. We were introduced and I was sufficiently impressed to stop squidging mud through my toes. Norman smiled at me; I blinked at him and went back to squidging mud. I was eleven years old.

After that, Norman Workman was around the house all the time. He must have liked the way I squidged mud or something, because he was seven years older than I and had a job and money in his jeans. But he would take me to the nicest places even when I was such a little girl. We went to Mt. Lowe and Catalina and the old Bostick Animal Farm. For me it was like going out with my grandpa, but it didn't bother Norman for he was always gentle and considerate and wonderful to be with. Then the First World War came along and Norman went off with the other young men.

We visited him at Fort Leavenworth where he was taking his training, and while we were there I began to get the idea he might be feeling *really* romantic about me. He didn't say anything, but I could tell. I had to laugh to myself about it, and I was excited, but mostly scared. I wanted to get married but I'd put the thought out of my mind because I felt that with my illnesses there wasn't any way in the world I could ever be a real wife.

As near as I can recall, my collapsing tendencies, and other major illnesses, began in grade school, shortly after my first attempt at heavier-than-air flight. This involved a schoolmate, Cecil, who maintained an enormous physical bulk by downing a loaf of bread and a full crock of creamy milk every day after classes. Cecil and I had been to see an air show and soon developed an uncontrollable urge to imitate the graceful soaring of the old crates we had seen. We lugged a big beach umbrella up to the steeple on our barn, where it was decided, at the last minute, that Cecil's girth was not ideal for a test pilot, so I was given the honor of the first jump.

I launched myself from the steeple and immediately shot toward the ground at slightly less than the speed of sound. I landed on my back across a saw-horse, then fell in a limp heap, while Cecil stared in moon-faced horror. The injuries I received in that aeronautical venture set up a chain reaction that kept me in hospitals, wheel chairs, and in bed at home for months at a time. Even today, if you were to run your finger ever so gently along my spine, I would probably scream wildly and spiral through the ceiling. Happily, it's unusual for people to run their fingers along anyone's spine, so I can generally avoid this excruciating pain.

A list of my other illnesses and accidents reads like a medical dictionary and sounds highly improbable; at this stage I am sometimes inclined to doubt some of it myself. When I was four I had scarlet fever and diphtheria in quick succession. That left me with weakened eyes and a throat obstruction. The obstruction was removed by surgery, but I then became blind and deaf and dumb. Sight and hearing came back gradually, and so did my voice, but in later years I used to lose it again occasionally. I've heard some remarks to the effect that this was a tidy little arrangement for the people who had to live with me. I've had kidney trouble, sinus trouble, and twice broke my arm cranking my father's Maxwell. I also broke my foot by stepping into a hole that shouldn't have been there. I

23

needn't go into detail about croup and colic, chicken pox and whooping cough, mumps and measles. I take those for granted.

Eventually Norman was shipped overseas and he was away for a year and a half. When he came back he asked me to marry him. "Why that's the craziest idea I ever heard in my life," I said, but I had the queerest drop-away feeling inside. "I'd make a fine wife, wouldn't I? Sick all the time. Why I'd never be able to keep a house running a week." Norman didn't keep asking. He just assumed our marriage as a fact. I even told him I could never have children and he said he knew all about that and there was no need to discuss it. I think what finally broke me was the quiet way he said one night, "I just want to be around you all the time and I'll do my best to take care of you."

Before the wedding we—or, rather, I—bought a house. Those were busy days, and since this house was a fairly familiar sight to me, I had not bothered to investigate the inside. From the outside it looked fine. The price was so low I had just grabbed at it and put down a deposit. When Norman (who somewhere along the line since then became "Pappy") asked me how many rooms there were, I had to admit I didn't know. When he asked what the place looked like inside, I waved my arms and said defensively, "Well . . . you know . . ." Actually, it was a wonderful little house, and, except for one small circumstance, it *was* a bargain. When we got the key and began our inspection tour we found that the old Frenchman who'd lived there had kept goats in the kitchen. Not one or two

24

goats but, judging from the available evidence, a whole flock or herd or whatever goats run around in.

We had to spend the week before our wedding cleaning the available evidence out of our bridal bower. This, I remember thinking as I stuck my head out the window for a breath of fresh air, is definitely not the way for a girl to begin her married life. Now I can see that it was not the way to begin just *any* old marriage, but for mine, as it turned out, it had a certain fitness.

Like every other girl, I have some fond memories of my wedding day, including the fact that Norman and I arrived about an hour late. But the most enduring one was provided by the fast thinking of my friend Ida Ewing. Ida was to play the piano, and at the last minute discovered she had not brought the music for the traditional "Here Comes the Bride." In bold desperation she closed her eyes and banged loudly away at the only tune she knew by heart. I came close to fainting when I heard the melody that was wafting me up the aisle, but ever since I have had an especially warm regard for "Oh, Dem Golden Slippers."

At breakfast, that first morning in the Kruse's kitchen, we heard what they thought of our plan to live on the Umpqua. "Why don't you get some sense into that empty head of yours?" Dad Kruse roared as he plowed his way through a plateful of bacon and eggs. "You ain't no farmer's wife and Pappy ain't no farmer. You'll all kill yourself over there at Scottsburg." Sniffed Mom Kruse: "Only

Heddens live over that way anyhow." The running controversy in the valley was over who had gotten there first in the pioneer days—the Heddens or the Applegates. Mom was of Applegate stock.

One of the sons, Fred Kruse, his blue eyes piercing, looked at me for a long time and then said, in his quick, flat way: "If you really want to live on that God-forsaken river, I've got three acres down there I got when Uncle Buck Applegate died. I'll give you that piece and you can build a house on it."

"We don't want it for nothing," I said, my heart jumping, "but it might be a good thing to buy. When can we see it?"

"Right now, if you want to," he answered.

It was late afternoon when we reached my valley. The vine maples were turning to brilliant scarlet, and the aspens and second growth alders were mellowing to gold. The sky was full of rushing gray clouds, and as we drove down the narrow highway we could see the huge firs gesturing to the breeze and smell the fragrance they spread on the air. The sun split the clouds somewhere far away and sent a long pink finger to color the mountain tops. Scattered everywhere were wild apple trees, covered with red apples so small and shiny they looked like Christmas tree ornaments. It seemed there were deer under almost every apple tree, munching the windfalls; they raised their heads, twitched their ears and looked incuriously as we passed. Once, not a hundred yards from the road, we saw five elk, as large as cattle, grazing watchfully in a meadow just at the line where forest fringed into field.

"There's bear around here, too," said Fred Kruse.

"You'll have to get Paul Applegate here in Scottsburg to take you hunting, Pappy. He's about the best there is in this country. Walks quiet as an Indian and he's a dead shot." Pappy, soaking up the look and smell of the valley, smiled wistfully. All at once, I got an indescribable feeling of well-being; I *knew* my decision to come to the Umpqua was right. In this magnificent valley Pappy would start to live again.

The highway wound gently among the towering firs, through tangles of wild currant and huckleberry, through graceful groves of myrtle and glades of waving ferns. Everywhere, the blackberry vines, stirred by the wind, writhed in leafy torment and sent out long tendrils to take over any unoccupied spot of land. The car stopped. "Here we are," said Fred. As the motor fell silent a jay screamed from an oak and was answered by the irritated chatter of a squirrel.

We got out of the car and stood looking at the river. "Hey," said Young Norman, "the river's running the wrong way." Fred looked up. "The wind comes from the ocean and riffles the surface upstream," he said. "It looks like that almost every afternoon. In the morning, it's so still you'd think it was a lake." We were silent then, watching the great, green stream, which was partly hidden by massive tree trunks and matted willows. "My land goes clear down to the river," explained Fred. "The rest of it's up there above the road. Up there'd be a good place to put a house."

"Let's go over and look at that old cabin," I suggested. As we approached the old shack we could see that it had a slight list toward the river. Under the trees, in the fading light, it looked somber and uninviting. "Who owns it?" I asked Fred.

"Nobody, I guess. It was put up back about 1927 for the men who dug the tunnel through the mountain. When the tunnel was finished, they just went away and left it here," he answered.

The door was ajar; it must have been ajar for a long time because it stood fast against my efforts to close it. Inside, the shack was dark. There was only one room, about twenty-two by twenty-six feet. There was a window at each end; one of them was half broken out and a hunter or someone had stuffed a dirty blanket into the break. The room was gaunt and empty. Rough, bare two-by-fours supported the siding, and the floor, pitted by loggers' caulked boots, tilted perilously toward the river. The place reeked of age and disuse and mustiness, but the pervading odor was the musk of strong perspiration and stronger tobacco smoke.

Suddenly Fred spoke up: "Gladys, why don't you just stay with us in Yoncalla and forget the whole thing. It's not too late; you still have some money left and you won't have a worry at the farm."

I turned to Young Norman: "What do you think? We could use this until we're ready to build a house. It'd take a little work, I know, but . . ."

"Let's not even talk about it," he answered dejectedly.

Suddenly a new voice spoke close to my ear: "You can't stay here tonight anyway," it said. I jumped about a foot and turned to see Paul Applegate standing behind me. No one had heard him come in. Paul was an old friend from my Oregon childhood. He was no longer young, but he still took a secret pride in appearing in his friends' houses as if he had materialized from the atmosphere. I've often wondered if any Indian ever moved as silently as he could. He lived with his wife, Maude, a short way down the road.

"Now, don't go and get excited," Paul soothed. "Maude wants you people to come down to the house and spend the night. You can't stay in this place."

I looked at Pappy's pale face and I looked at Young Norman. "All right, Paul," I accepted, "but just for tonight. And thanks." We drove over to the Applegate house and put Pappy to bed.

Young Norman took a long walk after supper. When he came back I asked, timidly, "Well, how do you like it?" He avoided my eyes and was silent for awhile. Then he gulped, "Well, the river's nice."

2

Show Me
to My Room

THE NEXT MORNING we sat around the big table in the Applegate's kitchen, sipping at mugs of steaming coffee. Maude Applegate, just over five feet tall, in her late thirties, neat and precise and positive, looked at me and I could tell she was warming up for speech. Maude does not stutter, but she seems to hesitate just before embarking on a sentence. Her conversation is punctuated by these moments, as though she were racing her mental motor before letting out the words. "You're not figuring on going back to that shack, are you?" she asked, "because if you are I might as well tell you you'll never make it. Why don't you all just stay here until you can get settled in a decent place?"

"I don't know of any decent place we could afford, do you?"

"No," answered Maude, "but that's no reason for your not staying here."

"I've got to get out and start looking for a job," said Young Norman, running his hand through his curly hair. "We've got to make a living."

Paul Applegate, leaning back in his chair, spare and relaxed, regarded us with amusement. "Making a living up here's about the easiest thing in the world," he said in his soft, pleasant voice. We perked up. "First thing is the blackberries," he said. "This country's got more blackberries than all the Christians and part of the heathen could eat. You can sell all the berries you want down at the cannery at Eugene and they pay good prices, too. Or, if you wanted, you could make blackberry jam and jelly and I'll bet you could sell all you could make." He regarded us soberly for a moment. Then, with a slow wink, he said, "Blackberry wine ain't bad for drinking, and I know you could sell a lot right around here. Of course, the folks up in the Capitol at Salem might not like it if the word got around. You'd have to keep it mighty quiet.

"Now, you take huckleberries. There ain't as many huckleberries as blackberries around here but they're free for the picking and city people like to buy huckleberries. The price is always high as can be. Another thing, and probably better than even blackberries, is to pick those bastard ferns that grow around here. The florists in California will buy all the fern and lemon leaf you can pick and it's a good business, too, because you can pick them all year 'round. Another thing to get in the woods is chittum bark, only usually just the kids go out for chittum. That's a kind of bark that grows on the buckthorn trees. The kids strip off the bark and let it dry. It's the stuff they make cascara sagrada out of. That's a physic."

32

Maude interrupted: "Don't let anybody give you any of that stuff. I chewed some once and I was on the dead run for the privy all day long."

"Of course," Paul continued, "all those things can be done with no capital, just a little gumption and sweat. Now, if you want to work a little harder, you can grow cucumbers for the pickle factory down at Reedsport or you can grow strawberries. This country grows some really nice strawberries. Or you could grow Bing cherries. They grow fine but, of course, nobody likes to pick cherries so maybe you'd be stuck with the crop. And I don't see why you couldn't catch a lot of salmon and smoke them the way the Indians used to do and sell that somewheres.

"The thing I'd do if I was you, though, would be to bootleg venison. City people are crazy for it. Go out at night and spotlight the deer. That way you can slaughter them. It's risky, but I'll bet you could make a lot of money that way." He grinned at the surprised expression on Pappy's face. "I'm just joking about that last," he said, gently.

"The funny thing is that nobody does any of the things I've been telling you about," Paul added.

"Why not?" asked Young Norman.

"Well, I'll tell you, young man," answered Paul. "There's just too damn much hunting and fishing to be done around here to allow a man time to go wrasslin' bastard ferns or blackberries out in the woods."

While Paul spoke, the room had darkened and Maude switched on the kitchen lights. It had started to rain, in the insidious way it does in Oregon. A few minutes before, the sun had been shining brightly. Then, with no show of emotion, no wind, no lightning or thunder, the rain began seeping down from the heavens, slowly, soundlessly, persistently and, I was to learn, endlessly. "We need it," said Paul. "It's been mighty dry around here this summer."

Sometimes the rain comes in gusty squalls and the fists of the storm bang against your house and make the flames in the fireplace shudder. At such times, the electric wires are blown down or sag beneath the weight of fallen boughs, and the telephone usually loses its voice for hours or days. But this morning, there were no theatrics. Just the soft, tiny droplets, making the road a ribbon of black sateen, turning the great trunks of firs into porphyry columns, polishing the leaves of the willows and graying the mountains into watery invisibility. After an hour or so of this hypnotic rain, the eaves begin to drip and a thousand rivulets carve their way to the river. From the kitchen I watched the Umpqua, far below, running slowly under a steamy white blanket of mist.

"Hey!" Young Norman suddenly shouted. "We'd better get down to that cabin and see if the roof leaks." For a moment, in the bright warmth of Maude's kitchen, I had forgotten the shack!

The roof leaked, but not as badly as we had expected. We flashed a light upward to the sharply-tilted roof and saw wide splotches of dampness where the rain had entered and soaked the old shingles. In several places, small puddles had formed on the floor and then skittered down the slope to the out-of-doors again.

The rain was stronger, now; real rain instead of the first

34

misty, drifting stuff. Young Norman leaned a ladder against the cabin and climbed to the slippery roof, pushing new shingles under the old ones. The rain poured off his hat and dripped relentlessly through his waterproof. He was a doleful sight against the gray sky, caught under the black overhang of the firs.

Paul, in his quiet voice, kept urging us to go back to Yoncalla, but every time I looked at Pappy I could see his health improving, and I knew the Umpqua was the place for us. It was now long past the six months the doctor had given Pappy to live. Apparently, Pappy did not have leukemia. He was probably suffering from a dye poisoning which affects the cells that manufacture blood, as does leukemia. The dye poisons can be eliminated, and gradually the blood-producing mechanism functions again.

"You're welcome to stay with us as long as you like," said Paul Applegate, "but if you decide to go back to Yoncalla, I'll be glad to buy your land. I've been wanting it ever since my daddy left it to Fred Kruse."

Paul's arguments were as encompassing as the rain. I don't know what my final answer to Paul might have been. Happily, there never was any need to decide whether to return to Yoncalla permanently. Claude Sherman made the difference, just as he had in El Monte. He drove over one day while we were trying to scrape the worst of the dirt from the cabin. In his usual methodical way, he glided along on his crutches, making a thorough inspection of the shack.

"You going to live in this, Gladys?" he asked.

"No," I replied, "we're just going to camp here until we can figure out how and where to build a house.

Paul's going to burn this old cabin when we're through with it. He's tired of looking at it." Claude did not say anything.

Later, at the Applegates, Claude spoke up. "That old cabin has some wonderful timbers in it, big heavy stuff," he said. "It would be a shame to burn it."

We thought that over for a while but no one had anything to say. Then Claude spoke again. "Why don't you hook a cat onto it and drag it over to your land?" he said. "Then you could fix it up and when you went to sell, you'd have something worth while to offer. Or you could rent it."

Paul became enthusiastic. "I'll tell you what I'll do," he said. "I'll advance the money you need to fix that cabin into a nice little house. Then, to pay you for your work, I'll let you have it rent-free for a year and a half. At the end of the year and a half, I'll buy your land, house and all. What do you think?"

That was the arrangement we finally made, and a few days later, in the evening when the traffic on the highway was lightest, some loggers threw a cable around the cabin and dragged it behind a big yellow tractor to our land. They set it down gently on a foundation of rocks, and the old place looked almost pretty on its new site in the falling dusk. Now that we had a plan, my spirits were soaring; I could see where we were going and the path looked promising. Paul and Young Norman found an old cook stove someone had thrown away and they pulled and pushed it into the shack. It had no legs, but Young Norman propped it up on rocks and cut a hole in the roof and installed stove pipes. We had no electricity, of course, and no running water and no sanitary facilities. But we had our sleeping bags and a cot from the Applegates. We hung a few blankets over the gaping windows (the second window had broken while the cabin was being moved), found some apple boxes which we set up for furniture, bought six pails for water, and moved in.

Immediately, we began drawing plans for the new house. The original shack would serve as a big living room. At each end we would build two parallel wings, one for a dining area, kitchen and screened porch, and the other for bedrooms and a bath. In the middle of the U we planned to build a den later, or another bedroom. Before long, the sweet-smelling lumber began to arrive from the mill, and our home on the Umpqua started to become a reality.

The local people, of course, visited us almost every day. There are only seventy-five families on our stretch of the Umpqua and all of them considered themselves neighbors, even if they lived fifteen or twenty miles away. They brought us home-made preserves, home-made bread, cakes and pies, and cheese. They also brought salmon, and beef and pork from home-bred cows and hogs. Part of neighborliness in the valley is knowing everything there is to know about everybody else and the neighbors also brought their curiosity. They asked, and we told them, why we had come to the valley and we poured out all our hopes and dreams. They looked at the shack, shook their heads and offered to put together a big neighborhood party to get the work done quickly. "We could get that thing finished in one day," they said, "and have a lot of fun besides." We thanked them and said we'd like to do it ourselves.

For a while, it seemed that every man who dropped in was named Norman—Norman Weatherly, Norman Compton, Norman Spence and Norman Rydell all paid their neighborly respects. With my own two, there probably hasn't been such a concentration of Normans since the Battle of Hastings. All the neighbors listened gravely to our plans, but you could tell they didn't think much of our chances. They all felt we'd be lucky to last six months. Being kindly people, this saddened them a little.

We also had visitors from farther away. Before we left California, I gaily told all our friends to drop in on us any time. Since it's about nine hundred miles from Los Angeles to Scottsburg, this is a pretty good drop-in —about like dropping in from New York to Chicago—and I didn't expect many takers for my offer. I should have known better.

The stream of visitors started almost as soon as we opened the indoor camping season in our shack. No one seemed to mind that we hadn't any electricity, or running water, or sanitary facilities. They were content to sit on the apple boxes and eat off tin plates. While visitors were around, work on the shack sometimes had to be ignored, but that didn't trouble us. Our first order of business was to get Pappy well.

One of the first to show up was my mother. Mama arrived, looked around the shack, and sighed heavily. She peered at the great outdoors and sighed again. She said to me, "You keep those bears and deer and things away from me, understand?" as though I was the head zoo keeper.

The day after she arrived, she collared Claude Sherman, had him build her a work table, and sent out the word: "I'm not going to traipse around in this wilderness, but if someone will pick me some blackberries, I'll make the cobblers. Right now, I'm going to make a cake if you'll all get out of here."

We were happy enough to leave the cabin. It was one of those wonderful, soft days when the river looks as though it *must* be warm enough for swimming. Several cars were parked just below the road and people were unloading bathing suits and picnic boxes. We walked toward the cars but were stopped by a really splendid scream from Mama. When we looked up, she was streaming through the hole where a door would be some day. She looked like a molting ghost. Her face was covered with flour and so were her hands and arms and she left a wispy trail of flour in the air as she ran. "In there," she shrieked, gesturing toward the cabin. One man picked up a tire iron, a young lady hefted a Coke bottle by the neck, another girl snatched up a beach towel. All of them pounded toward the house, with me in the rear.

When I reached the kitchen, the warriors were standing in an awed circle. The girl with the towel was poised on her toes, legs spread, knees bent slightly, holding the beach towel like a matador's cape. There was a deep silence as a three foot snake, covered with flour and seething with humiliation, made his albino-ish way across the floor. "That's a great cake mix," said one of the men. Mama said later she was minding her own business when the snake dropped out of the rafters right into the bowl of cake batter. "I let him have a handfull of dough right in his face and then I got out," she said. The snake was harmless, we discovered later, but Young Norman scouted the rafters and chased out three more. Mama sighed again and went back to the city.

We had other animal visitors and we enjoyed them almost as much as the people. For instance, there was Sammy the cat. Sammy was a rake and a roamer with a wild eye and a devil-may-care tilt to his gray head. He belonged to a neighbor, but he appointed himself general superintendent of construction at our place and watched every move Claude and Young Norman made. Sammy was also a great comfort, in his gruff way, to Susie and the other cats we brought from El Monte. (I realize now I have not said anything about our cats. This is something like Noah descending from the ark and not mentioning animals. We have cats. Striped cats, Manx cats, gray cats, yellow cats. We have always had cats and I suppose always will. There was a time we had twenty-three of the creatures at once.)

Susie was a city cat, used to central heating, electricity, television, intimate candle-lit dinners, and the bright chatter of cocktail parties. In a word, Susie was neurotic. The wilds of the Umpqua scared her to death. She cried piteously at the sight of a deer and shuddered at every unusual sound. She was, naturally, a pushover for Sammy, who gathered this frightened bundle of nerves to his swaggering bosom and had her with kitten before we could warn her about the perils of country life.

Joe Jensen, an old friend of Pappy's from California,

showed up one day slavering for fishing and hunting. I was a bit apprehensive when Mr. Jensen appeared because he is a fellow who likes his comfort; I did not know how he would react to kerosene lanterns, tin plates and the blanket we had hung until we could get a new front door. I needn't have worried. Like the true gentleman he is, he took our primitive accommodations in stride. "I expected to sleep out doors," he said. "This is real luxury." We had fish and small game to eat and the evenings were warm; the old wood stove simmered along cozily and the kerosene lamps threw intricate shadows on the wall. We hated to see Joe Jensen go and he was not too happy about the prospect of another year at his desk. "Best time I ever had," he said. We were pleased, of course, but we had no idea he would continue to sing our praises when he got back to California. What he went around saying was something like this, "I've been hunting and fishing all over the West, but, even at twenty-five dollars a day, I've never had such a time as I did with the Workmans." That "twenty-five dollars a day" was pure rhetoric, of course; he was a guest.

We did not know we had a self-appointed press agent, and it would not have made any difference anyway because Pappy suddenly began to feel much worse. We scurried him down to the hospital at North Bend and the doctors pumped him full of miracle drugs. Apparently, it was an off day for miracles, because all Pappy got out of it was a dinger of a penicillin reaction. His face broke out in big, watery blisters and we kept plastering gauze on him until he looked like a badly-made snow man.

Work progressed slowly on the shack. Claude Sherman

41

and Young Norman had completed the service porch, all except for the screening; but with the waist-high walls in, we felt we had passed a major milestone. We were sitting around slothfully after supper one evening, congratulating ourselves, when we heard a car pause and then groan up the short pitch from the road to the cabin. There was a knocking on the wall. "See who's at the blanket," I said to Young Norman, but before he could reach it, a young man and a very attractive girl ducked in and stood contemplating us. With dismay, I might add, and other things starting with "d" including distaste and, possibly, disgust.

He was dressed like the second floor of Abercrombie and Fitch—the compleat sportsman—and carried two suitcases and a variety of aluminum tubes containing fishing rods. She was tall and willowy with the biggest brown eyes, set in a cool, everybody-says-I'm-beautiful face. She clutched herself tightly in a fur coat—to avoid contamination, I guessed. Her brown eyes gave me a quick, cool inventory: dumpy old lady in a faded wash dress, white hair a bit on the ratty side, heavy work shoes. "Here's a dolly I could learn to dislike in a hurry," I thought. I saw her eyes flick to the row of milk pails along the wall, shift to the apple-box furniture and Claude's crutches. When her eyes focused on Pappy, she gave a little cry and turned to her husband. "Jeee-sus," she said. It was sort of a prayer. I couldn't blame her, really. Sitting there in the shadows which our kerosene lamps threw out instead of light, Pappy, with his penicillin reaction all over his face, looked like the second monster from the right in the latest horror movie.

"Well, here we are," said the man in a valiant try for cheeriness. Pappy and Young Norman and Claude and I chewed on that for a while. Incontrovertible. No question about it. They were here. With us.

"Won't you come in?" I said graciously, which was pretty bright of me since they were standing in the middle of the room. "I mean, won't you have a cup of coffee?"

"Coffee!" She practically spit the word out. "We've driven all the way from San Francisco. I want food."

Claude jumped up, balanced himself on his leg and pushed his apple box toward the girl, giving it quite a bit of Old World courtesy. "Won't you have my chair?" he asked. She looked at Claude as though he had just offered her the hot seat at Sing Sing.

"I could make up some sandwiches," I volunteered. "There isn't much in the house."

"I want more than sandwiches," said my new friend.

"I *have* got a few catfish," I said, "I. . . ."

"Catfish!" cried Mr. Abercrombie-and-Fitch. "How about catching my own?"

"You want to fish at this time of night?" asked his lady.

"Sure," he said. "Catfish don't bite in the daytime. I came up here to fish and I might as well get started."

I looked at Young Norman. He grinned and shrugged his shoulders. "I'll show you a backwater where we always get catfish," he said. "Come along."

"You're not really going?" wailed the girl. Her voice trailed off into a moaning "Ohhh" as he ducked out through the blanket into the bright moonlight. She sat down abruptly on one of the suitcases, buried her head in mink and sobbed. Pappy and Claude Sherman, the cowards, faded away. I wasn't sure how you go about comforting an iceberg, but I figured it was up to me so I laid a motherly paw on her furry shoulder and made cooing noises. I was rewarded with a shrug and decided to let her wallow in her misery. When she stopped sobbing and raised her face, I was happy to see her mascara had run beautifully.

"It's so wild," she said at last, in a pitifully small voice, "so wild and scary. The woods are full of animals, wolves and bears and mountain lions. . . ."

"Nonsense," I interrupted. "There aren't any wolves or mountain lions. There are a few bears but we *like* to have them around to remind us the country is still country."

This set her off again. "Bears," she whimpered. "I knew it. I knew there would be bears." The poor thing was really frightened; I began to feel sorry for her. She did not make it easy. She was quiet for a while and then she said, "I'm terribly tired. Could you show me to the bathroom?"

"Bathroom?" I said as though I'd never heard the word. "We don't have a bath. We don't have plumbing of any kind." She gave me a stricken look. "We—uh—go outside," I said.

She drew her mink a bit tighter. "Then show me to my room," she said. "I'm going to bed."

"We don't have any room except the one we're in," I said. "The other rooms aren't finished yet. But we do have plenty of sleeping bags and you're welcome to those."

I don't know what she might have said to that because a tree branch clattered to the roof and her head came up with a jerk and a gasp. In that split second, Sammy, the big gray cat, elected to enter the room. He hurtled through the window flap like he'd traded in his tail for a rocket, splayed out on the floor like those pictures of flying squirrels, bounced into the girl's lap and shot back of the stove where Susie started telling him off for a no-good, two-timing, philandering Tom.

"A lion," my client yelled. "Lions! Lions!" She zoomed off the suitcase as though it was a catapult and streamed into my arms. She screamed and then she stopped screaming and trembled for a while. She had just straightened up and let go of me when Paul Applegate coalesced in front of her. "You're new here, aren't you?" he asked cheerily, and she leaped into the protection of my motherly arms again. We were standing like that, the lady sobbing and shaking and Paul Applegate patting her shoulder in an ineffectual way, when the men returned, jubilant over their catch of a dozen catfish. When she saw her husband, the girl began to gulp in great gasps of air as though she had been under water for a long time. Then, calling on the deep inner reserves which make us women such wonderful creatures, she gradually decided to live again.

The men fried a batch of catfish and downed them amid general congratulations. The lady sipped wanly at coffee. They could not eat all the fish so Claude put the left-overs on a platter and took them to the half-walled service porch. He put a dishpan over the platter and laid a large rock on the dishpan to keep the cats away. Then we all inserted ourselves into sleeping bags and peace descended on the dilapidated manse.

At about three o'clock in the morning, the sylvan calm split open and shattered into ten thousand ragged jets of sound. One moment all was calm, all was bright, and the next second we were in the midst of a screaming, scratching, howling maelstrom of noise. One frightened cat can make a fantastic amount of noise; five frightened cats can generate eighteen or twenty times as much, screeching high notes which would make Dizzie Gillespie weep into his goatee. Under the cat howls, we could hear the tinny banging of the dishpan.

"Holy Mother Machree," cried Young Norman, lurching to his feet, still half asleep. Claude could not find his crutch and stood in one spot, hopping and cursing softly. Our lady visitor screamed. Young Norman and I dashed for the blanket leading to the service porch. The porch was a solid blur of cats. In their sincere panic, the cats were tearing around the porch, spinning around and around and climbing higher and higher on the walls as they whirled by. When they reached the top, they splayed out and over into the night, hurled off the porch by centrifugal force. As they went into orbit, their squalls trailed off. Suddenly all was quiet.

In the moonlight, we saw the cause of it all. A bear cub was sitting on the floor, happily chewing away on a catfish and holding another in his right paw like an ice cream cone.

"Bears!" I shouted, dropping the blanket over the doorway. Our lady screamed again. Claude and Norman banged on pans to scare the cub away. By the time I got a lamp lit, our visitors were stuffing their clothing into the suitcases. The lady was trembling so hard I thought she'd vibrate right out of her fur coat which she had put on over her nightgown. Her husband had stuffed his pants on over his pajamas. They threw their gear into their car, started the engine and began to back out.

"Wait," I cried, "wait." The man let the engine idle as I went up to the car. "Look," I said, "just tell me one thing. How'd you happen to stop in here?"

"Joe Jensen told us about you," he said. "Jensen said he'd never had such a good time. Now *you* tell me one thing. Where do you get the nerve to charge twenty-five dollars a day for a dump like this?" The car rolled down the hill, reached the road, and roared out of sight.

I went back into the shack. "You know what they thought?" I said. "They thought we were going to charge them twenty-five dollars a day from something Joe Jensen said."

Pappy handed me a steaming cup of coffee.

"Twenty-five dollars?" he mused. "You should have made them pay. I don't know anywhere in the world you could get a night like tonight for a measly twenty-five dollars."

It was hard to tell just where we were living in those early days. We were sleeping in the single room of the slowly expanding cabin, but I was fighting a losing battle with the wood stove and we ate most of our meals at the Applegate's.

We were nosing around in the Applegate's kitchen one day, looking for something to cook for supper, when Maude said, "Come on. Let's go down to the store; I need a few things."

"Store?" I asked. "What store?"

47

"Hedden's," she answered. "It's just down the road a couple of miles."

Hedden's store! If she'd said we were going to Heaven I don't think I could have been more pleased. This was the store the old pioneer, Cyrus Hedden, had operated, the first store in southern Oregon. As a child I had heard over and over again from my father about Cyrus Hedden. In the long hours I'd spent in bed as a little girl, I'd woven my romances about old Cyrus plodding through the primitive Oregon forests, just ahead of a band of bloodthirsty Indians, dragging a friend who'd been struck in the stomach by an arrow. Emma Hedden, Cyrus' granddaughter, was in my romances too—the tough but motherly ruler of the cleancut lumberjacks, the loggers who moved about in the dark woods and who skipped with lightfooted grace from log to log in the churning rivers.

I don't know clearly what I expected to find in Emma Hedden's store or in Emma herself, but I was excited when Maude and I walked in. The store itself could have been lifted from any television western: a false front facing the highway, big windows on either side of the central door. It sat stolidly between Grange Hall and the little community church. Across the street was the beer parlor and a few houses. That was Scottsburg.

Emma Hedden was behind the row of post office boxes to the right of the door when we arrived, a medium-sized, mild-appearing, handsome woman with graying hair and small, old-fashioned glasses. The store was white inside, with a high ceiling, and at first glance seemed understocked. But then I realized Emma had a bit of just about anything needed in Scottsburg. Shiny galvanized

48

buckets gleamed from a high shelf. There were horsecollars and hammers, a few bolts of cloth, and stacks of Levis counterpoised against a basket of bright orange oranges. A curl of weathered fly paper spiraled down, coated with fossilized flies. There were watches and wrenches, razor blades, thread, bathing caps, sponges, hickory shirts, cap guns, gloves and toys.

An old pug dog was lying among loaves of bread stacked on a low counter directly opposite the door, and fresh country milk, in half-gallon and gallon jars, was aligned along one side of the room. There was no refrigeration; no slightest hint of the supermarket; the store smelled of leather and cookies and prunes and oil and bananas all at once. Behind the counter where Emma stood, an array of familiar labels on cans and boxes stood stiffly on the shelves, but they seemed incongruous there. There were no vegetables at all, only the oranges and six or seven tired lemons. Emma Hedden came slowly from behind the counter. "This is Gladys Workman," Maude said. "She is going to live here."

"Yes, I heard," said Emma.

To me, she said, "How do you do?" That was all. I was a little disappointed. Just "How do you do?" Not "Welcome to Scottsburg," or even "You look like an old Indian I used to know." Here was Emma, one of my heroines, and all she could say to me was the meekest kind of "How do you do?" Maude and Emma had already resumed a conversation which must have been running for years. I felt a little left out but I caught snatches of talk. Who was sick. Who had been to Eugene (the nearest large town, seventy-eight miles to the northeast). Plans for a pot luck.

Somebody who lived "up on the hill" had died. ("The damned old fool," Emma said, "he should've died. He wouldn't do anything anybody told him to do.") A cow had died. ("I wouldn't put it past him to have shot her himself, he's such an ornery old cuss.") A baby had been born during the night. (Maude: "How is she?" Emma: "I was up there first thing this morning and she's fine. Got a girl this time." Me: "Did she have it at home?" Emma and Maude gave me long looks, one apiece. Emma: "Sure she had it at home. Where'd you think she'd have it?")

There'd been a fight the night before at the beer parlor across the highway from Emma's store. Two women had screamed and kicked and torn at each other until they fell into a deep hole. Then they had been pulled out and had ganged up on the man who was the cause of it all. Emma had been summoned to break up the fight. "Both of them claimed he'd been two-timing them," said Emma. "Who was it?" asked Maude. "I don't think you know them," said Emma. "One of them's called Kitty, sort of short and fattish, and the other's a tall redhead called Jeanie, from Drain. Kitty was bleeding like a stuck pig but she wasn't really hurt. I sent them all home to sleep off their beer."

I felt a little queasy. I'd never been in a place where women fought in beer parlors and fell into holes alongside the highway. What kind of a place was this Scottsburg, anyway? In my dreams I had pictured the quiet rural community, a peaceful settlement, filled with the prosperous, happy and benevolent descendants of the rugged covered-wagon pioneers. Instead, I heard Emma saying: "There was another mess at the loggers' camp last night, too. I'm going to have to go down there and clean the whole lot of them out, you'll see."

We left the store and climbed into the car. Maude pointed across the highway to an old off-white house sitting comfortably in a yard billowing with sunflowers. "That's Emma's house," Maude said. "She lives there all alone with about twenty dogs. She sure loves those dogs. Old Gard Sagaberd helps her out in the yard and he opens the store for her in the morning and starts the fires."

I nodded absently. My mind was on the fighting. The more I thought about it, the more queasy I got. "Do they always send for Emma to break up the fights?" I asked.

"Yes," said Maude. She laughed. "Emma's the voice of authority around here."

"What I don't understand is how a little gray-haired lady like that can stop a couple of drunk loggers from fighting," I said.

"It's just Emma," Maude said. "She can do it. I guess nobody's going to hit her, and if they swing they'll sure hit her because she's right in the middle. She just says, 'Damn it, now, you fellows get the hell out of here and sober up.' And they go. Sometimes she might have to stomp on their feet a little—and that hurts like the dickens—but they always do what she says."

"Isn't there a policeman in Scottsburg?" I asked.

"No," Maude replied. "I guess Emma's the only real policeman we have. She can scare any man in the valley when she's got a sad iron in her hand. There's a deputy sheriff down at Reedsport, but even if you could get him, he probably wouldn't arrive until the next day."

We rode for a while, under the canopy of the forest.

"Golly, Maude, what kind of people are they, anyway?"

"Oh, they're just drifters," Maude said. "The men come in for the logging season and there's always a bunch of women with them. The loggers get drunk 'most every night and raise a little hell."

"Boy, I'm sure off the track," I said. "My romancing is running in reverse. I thought most loggers were college boys working in the woods to help pay for their education. I read about that somewhere."

Maude slowed the car and looked at me in awe. "Honest to God," she said, "I don't know what kind of stuff you read but you've sure got a hell of a lot to learn."

3

Like a Bloody
Roman Emperor

THERE WERE ONLY two kinds of people in the valley—
the Old Timers and the Drifters. Pappy and Norman
and I did not count; we were temporary. "They'll be on
the county in six months," everyone said, "and then they'll
get out." The Drifters didn't count either; they came in
the summer to work in the woods, and then disappeared.
While they were there, they made the valley night seem
like some ghastly Halloween and the Old Timers cursed
them and were glad to see them leave.

The Old Timers were the elite and they could do no
wrong. When one of the more passionate members of the
younger generation opened her bedroom to a new logger,
the Old Timers knew it almost as soon as the lucky fellow
himself. But never a harsh word against her. She came
from an Old Timer family and they tolerated her hobby.
When Dud got drunk, which he did with commendable
fidelity, and ran his car into a bridgehead, leaving the

highway strewn with splintered guard rails, the Old Timers chuckled. "Don't know how long the county can afford Ol' Dud," they winked. "Those bridges are pretty expensive."

They nodded in agreement with one calico-covered *grande dame* of the hills: the old lady had agreed to pay for a modern home where she was to live with her daughter and son-in-law. While the building progressed, she stayed with her cabin in the forest, her privy and her kerosene lamps. When she first saw the new house, the framing was up, the roof was on and she noticed a tangle of black soil pipes.

"What are those things?" she asked.

"Those are for the plumbing," said her son-in-law. "They'll carry away the waste water from the bathtubs and the sink and the toilets."

"Toilets!" shrilled the old lady. "You mean you're going to put a privy in the house?"

"Not a privy," he said. "Toilets." He explained the admirable principles of the water reservoir, the flushing system, the porcelain base and the pipes under ground. The old lady listened and then delivered her ultimatum.

"There ain't," she said grimly, "going to be any privy in my house." Today, the unfinished house stands just as it did the day the old lady went back to her cabin in the hills. Except that rains have weathered the studding and blackberries are inching up toward the roof.

When we arrived in the valley, it was the Old Timers against the outside world, a world they scarcely believed existed. The valley was their world and the world was the valley. They had lived there forever. Their parents had lived there before them and some of their grandparents had turned the first earth along the Umpqua. They lived close to the soil and the winds and the drifting clouds; they knew the ways of the winds and of the river. And they knew positively and in harrowing detail absolutely everything about everybody—down to how long you wore a pair of socks and, I do not doubt, your current standing with the income tax man, the bank, and God.

They did not much like what they knew about us. Norman Workman and Young Norman Jackson were all right, but everyone knew "Norman Workman's wife" was unfit for life in the valley. They knew it was my brainstorm that had dumped us in their valley. They knew I had bought Fred Kruse's land and had arranged for the cabin to be dragged to it. "That damn fool woman," they said. "Even a city woman ought to have sense enough to know you can't live in a place like that and expect a sick man to make a living here."

I was enjoying the valley so much—watching Pappy get really well after his penicillin reaction and watching the cabin putting on such elegances as windows and doors —I did not know I was making a name for myself. Sometimes the valley evenings would be filled with towering pink clouds, and when that happened the river would look like strawberry ice cream and the dark green firs would take on an improbable reddish glow. In the stillness, I would watch deer shimmering out of the woods and listen to the soft calling of the doves. Coons sniffed around for table scraps and, in the dusk, an owl would hoot sharply. I was trying on the valley for size and I thought it was just about a perfect fit. What I did not know was that I did not fit the valley.

When visitors arrived from outside, I'd greet them happily and, for me, normally. I'd kiss the ladies and the men, too, in a flood of "dears" and "darlings." The valley, which could laugh juicily about the latest seduction down the river, was shocked by my behavior. "Kissed that fellow right there, right in front of Workman," they said. "If I had a woman like that, I'd beat the skin off her. Course, Workman's been sick, but even so . . ." When valley people dropped in, I'd introduce them to my friends. Some of them were from Hollywood and I'd say so, just as you'd say a fellow was from Seattle or Toledo. It never occurred to me the valley people would think I was name-dropping. Patty and George Hackett arrived and I introduced him as musical director of the Ice Follies. That's what he is, but the valley people thought I was making it up to impress them. "Meet Herb Pickup," I'd say. "He's up here from Hollywood where he works for Technicolor." I heard later what a terrible liar everyone thought I was. "Why would people from Hollywood want to come up here and visit in a shack like that?" they said.

My first gesture toward being a good neighbor blew up in my face. I invited a next-door neighbor's kids in for a party and slaved for days making decorations. The chief work was a gigantic spider web and the idea was to let the kids unravel it and win prizes as they went. Pappy and I worked two days putting it together. On the day of the party, everything was set: the pies were baked, ice cream was ready, and the soda pop was cooling. We waited expectantly for the guests to arrive. I was looking out the front window for the eightieth time when I saw the children being bundled into a car by their mother. I went out. "Aren't the children coming to the party?" I called. "They can't come today," she replied. I walked over to the car. "Joan was bad," the mother said, "and when one of them's bad, all of them get punished. None of them is going to the party." She must have noticed my face collapse, for she added, "These aren't city kids, Mrs. Workman. These are country kids and we raise them strict."

While I was the mover and shaker in getting us into the valley, from time to time I simply conked out. I guess my heart was still attacking. When that happened, I'd go down to Yoncalla for some good, solid rest and leave the Normans to batch it. This was the final, inexcusable, compounded, hydramatic SIN. Women in the valley do not let their men fend for themselves. The idea is to get up at four in the morning and warp out a hearty breakfast and then spend the rest of the day producing a hearty dinner and a hearty supper. Then word got around that Norman sometimes brought me coffee in bed in the morning. That did it! I was spoiled! A snooty, name-dropping show-off. "What the hell's she come up here for?" Emma Hedden asked rhetorically in her spindly voice. "She's always dressed up like she was somebody special and she even goes to the beauty parlor at Coos Bay. She won't even stay put. Goes running down to Yoncalla all the time. If she don't like it here, why don't she leave?" That about summed up my impregnable place in the hearts of the valley.

When Susie, the striped cat, got sick, I took her to a veterinarian. "That justs beats everything I've ever seen," said Maude Applegate. "Every cat in the valley has kittens twice a year and you can get all the cats you want. But no, that Gladys, who lives in a house with no windows or doors, has to show off—spending money on a sick cat." Agnes Hudson, who ran the party telephone line, did not help either. When people called us in the morning, she would say out of the goodness of her great heart, "No, sir. I'm not going to ring them this early. They don't get up until ten o'clock. Call back later." In bed until ten! Everyone knows that people who lie abed after the sun is up are immoral.

The first slight shiver of my status trickled into my mind during our initial visit to the Grange in the big white, steepled building that used to be the Scottsburg school.

Norman and I entered a very large room, barred near the door by a sort of picket partition which, I learned later, was the station of the Grange officer who guards the portals. Against what, no one said. We got past the guard all right and then had a simply wonderful ten minutes standing alone, completely ignored. One thing I can say about valley people: when they don't talk to you, you get a pretty fair idea of what not being talked to is like. The ladies were in cotton dresses and, mostly, in moccasin shoes; they wore no makeup and their hair ran to buns in the back or, in a few cases, to elaborate piled-up braids. The men wore Levis or khaki trousers and plaid mackinaws. Across the room there was an enormous cylindrical stove and next to it a big roll-top desk. In the right-hand corner was an old upright piano. There were no chairs, but around the walls there were benches. I was running through the multiplication table for amusement and had got to eleven times seven when Maude Applegate came along and introduced me to some of the ladies. "How do you do?" the lady said. "How do you do?" I said. Then we both meditated on the limpid beauty of the phrase as we stood in an icy sort of trance. (Eleven times seven is seventy-seven.) "You done any canning yet?" asked the lady, eyeing my print silk dress.

"No," I said.

"Peaches is good now," she said, drifting away. "Cheap, too."

I was introduced to Mary Levenhagen, a great mountainous woman who sat with her dumpling hands crossed where a lap would ordinarily be expected but where Mary had built up a bulge. Mary gave me a tired smile, followed by a delicate burp. Sitting next to her was Sadie Andrews, a tiny, hump-backed lady. They did not have much to say to me, but as I turned to meet the rest, I heard Mary say happily: "That man of mine shot me nine blue jays today. I sure hate those bastardly birds."

Jane Murphy howdedoed me and remarked she was just back from Pomona. My heart warmed, for at last I was on solid ground. I knew a lot of people in Pomona and I fired off a salvo of names and, almost immediately, fell back in considerable disorder. Jane Murphy was not talking about Pomona, California; *her* Pomona was the county Grange.

I met some of the men, too, especially Jimmy Van Natta. "Hi," he said in his breezy way. "I know all about you. You're the snooty old gal up from California. Some of the girls were telling me you wore gloves when you went to club the other day." He patted my shoulder. "Don't worry about it," he said. "Mae, my wife, had gloves when we came up here. Yours will wear out fast."

There was some sort of entertainment and then the Grangers charged a long, trestle-like table loaded with food. I ate until I felt my eyes bugging out. Then I discreetly asked one of my new friends where the ladies' room was. She pointed and I got under way. Just as I got to the door, a man came out. "Go on in," he said. "There ain't but one and we all use it." Splendid arrangement, I thought. I went in and backed right out. I did not like dirty bathrooms then and I do not like dirty bathrooms now. I made no outcry; I just backed out; but every eye in the house was zeroed in on me.

Next day, Maggie Burton dropped around. ("I'm Margaret Burton," Maggie says, but she's always called Maggie.) "I want to tell you something, Gladys, I hate to do it, but you ought to know. It's about Grange last night." Memories of that enchanted evening swam through my head like visions of sugar plums. Maggie continued, "One of the ladies said you were sort of stand-offish and wouldn't talk to anyone. And when they served the food, you just minced around and hardly ate anything at all."

"Stop!" I cried. "I ate like a bloody Roman emperor!"

Maggie ignored me. "It's not a friendly thing to pick at your food," she said. "And the way you went on about the bathroom. Well! You'll just have to learn to accept things like that. You're not in the city any more."

Not long after, Pappy picked up the party line telephone just in time to hear ". . . that Workman woman? I wouldn't bother about her. She's crazy as a chicken with its head off. Did you hear about the way she acted at Grange?"

Pappy interrupted angrily, "Gladys isn't crazy. It's just that she's been sick and she's not used to your ways yet."

"Sick," sniffed the voice. "Of course, you'd have to say that. She's sick all right. Sick in the head."

Pappy was mad about it, but I was not. "I just don't think I understand these people," I said. "Everything I do seems to go sour."

"Maybe you're trying too hard," Pappy said gently. The events of my life in the valley flicked through my mind; I tried to see them the way the valley people would. Maybe, I thought, I *am* a little nutty. Maybe there was enough there to justify the local diagnosis. Especially when I recalled "the night Gladys tried to kill us all with poisoned clams and darn near made it."

Maude Applegate, who knows the names of all the plants and trees and about salmon in the river and the best time to pick berries and hazel nuts, started the whole thing when she called across the road, "Come on, Gladys. We're all going clamming down at Reedsport. Put on a pair of slacks and let's get going." I do not have a pair of slacks because I have a theory that the parts of me which go into slacks are too broad for such apparel, but Maude insisted and shoe-horned me into an old pair of Levis.

61

They were three sizes too small and I had bad trouble sitting down in the car. When I did get sat down I could feel the stiff denim rubbing all the skin off my knees.

I was seeing the lower river for the first time. The narrow road wound along sheer granite cliffs which were covered with the palest green fern fronds growing horizontally toward the river. The river itself, always close to the road, was as still as a lake and the many greens and yellows of the forest and the shifting clouds were reflected in its surface like some expert finger painting. At Reedsport, we got out at Heyes's Wharf and were looking at the weathered pilings, the mounds of chittum bark and the crab pots when Old Man Heyes came up.

"You see that in the paper about the red tide?" he asked me.

"What's the red tide?" I asked carefully, thinking he was about to use me as a straight man.

"It's a time when the water gets all red," he said. "I don't know what causes it, but it makes the clams poisonous."

The others called to me that the boat was ready; I said goodby to Old Man Heyes and laughed: "Well, it looks like a nice blue-green today, so I guess we're safe."

Maude hustled us into a power launch and we chugged away toward the sandbanks where the most succulent clams were supposed to lie. We spent a couple of hours in the wet sand, digging whenever we saw a clam hole or a little geyser of sandy water. By the time we had two sacks full of the big, juicy-looking clams, the wind was rasping at our faces and the waves were slapping and slurping over the sand flats.

The next night we had a party at our cabin, under our new electric lights—the first gaiety we'd had since reaching the Umpqua. Besides the Applegates, we had invited Jane and Ken Murphy ("Take it from a man who's swum to the headwaters of Old Fitzgerald," Ken declaimed as he tossed off his first glass, "don't ever pour water on the fire this stuff starts"), Dorothy and Walter Palmer, Maggie and Harry Burton, and Rock Freyer. We were all bubbling as we sat down to fried and steamed clams, crawdads, little potatoes with parsley butter, a cabbage salad, and Jane Murphy's famous rhubarb pie.

When the clams had disappeared, we were sitting at the table nibbling and picking, too full to think of doing the dishes, when Maude leaned over to me. "Don't Rock Freyer look sort of funny to you?" she asked. "He always looks funny to me," I answered, "with that big knobby face and the way his mouth sucks in when he doesn't wear his teeth."

"No, not that," Maude said. "Look at him. He's so pale." Rock Freyer's bumpy face, which was usually tanned and ruddy, was as white as a pile of gravel. He always spoke softly, but now we could scarcely hear him.

"I feel just terrible," he moaned. "I've got the worst pain in my stomach I've ever had. I better go."

"I don't think he ought to drive that old car when he feels so bad," I said. "He ought to take something." Then the awful thought struck me:

"The red tide!" I screamed, and then excitedly told them what Old Man Heyes had said.

"Well, damn it to hell," drawled Ken Murphy. "If the clams were poison, why'd you go ahead and cook them?" That was the only outburst. None of us felt anything but very full of food. We sat there and watched Rock suffer and waited for our own pains to start. Young Norman was solemn and silent. Maude and Paul Applegate stared bleakly at one another. Maggie Burton stared at the clamshells on her plate and Harry stared at her. I felt hot and then cold and waited for the poison to bite in.

"We better give Rock something," said Pappy (who had eaten no clams). "I'll get some warm soda water." With a sickly look, Rock downed five glasses of hot water with baking soda mixed in. Then he walked, listing slightly, toward the bathroom. Rock looked awfully sick. "Don't you think we ought to get a doctor?" someone suggested, and I went to the phone. I got Agnes Hudson. "Oh Agnes," I wailed, "see if you can get us a doctor. I think we've all eaten poisoned clams."

That was the end of the calm and dignity. The phone began to jangle. "Don't take soda water," someone on the party line said. "Take hot salt water. That'll make you throw up." It rang again. "I heard about the clams," a voice said. "I'll be right up with the best thing there is." Amid the clanging of the telephone bell, Paul Applegate turned green. "Maude, the poison's struck in on me and my stomach hurts like fire."

"Salt water, quick!" cried Maude, and Paul sucked down four glasses of hot salt water, got a funny look on his face, and dashed for the bathroom just as Rock Freyer came out. Pappy handed Rock a glass of salt water and Rock wanly started to swallow.

The pains were now generally contagious. "I feel

awful," cried Maggie Burton. "Give me some of that salt."
I noted the first twitches of pain in my stomach. Harry
Burton was very pale. "Whites of eggs," screamed the
party line. "Swallow all the egg whites you can." We had a
new crate of fifteen dozen eggs and four of us started
separating whites from yolks. As fast as we'd get a glass
of the dreadful stuff together, some sufferer would down
it. Egg shells almost filled the sink and yellow yolks
stared at us from a dozen pans. I downed a glass of egg
white, and after that the hot salt water tasted almost good. The phone rang again just as Pansy Andrews
rushed in the front door. "Mix the salt water and the soda
water," shouted the phone. "I got chittum bark to boil,"
cried Pansy. "It'll clear the poison out the bowels." Someone started chittum bark to boiling. By now, we all had
pains gripping our stomachs and all of us were belting
whites of egg, salt and soda water as fast as Pappy could
heat water. The phone rang again and it was Agnes Hudson. "I got hold of Dr. Sather," she said. "He says to take
plaster off the walls and mix it with water. He says it's
the best thing there is." This was capital information to
have—except there wasn't a house in the valley with plas-
tered walls.

Walter Palmer, usually so calm and steady, just went
to pieces. "I just remembered clams and whiskey is the
worst combination a man can take," he said, "and the
Lord knows I've had my share of both." He tried every
prescription off the party line before anyone else.

Rock Freyer was nibbling on a glass of bitter chittum
water when Roy Lewis burst in. "I heard about it on the
party line," he shouted. "I've got just the stuff. Old H&H.

It'll cure anything." He waved the bottle of dark amber liquid which was the valley nostrum for every ailment of man or beast. (Every valley home had a bottle of H&H on hand. It was good—five drops on a teaspoonful of sugar—for colds and colic; farmers rubbed it on cows to cure milk fever, a sniff would cure a headache, a few drops in hot water was good to soak your feet in to ease bunions. It was fiery hot and was generally known as old Hotter'n Hell.) "Give me some of that," sighed Rock. "I feel worse and worse."

The salt water was fantastically effective. You'd drink a few glasses and nothing would happen except you'd feel pumped up full. Then, so suddenly you could scarcely believe it, the salt water started its return trip at about the velocity of light. It was explosive and uncontrollable. The little cabin was rocking as though it were under an artillery barrage. Howitzer blasts of salt water and egg white and old H&H roared out the windows and sounded from the rear of the house. A Big Bertha exploded in the bathroom as the internal fireworks rumbled and exploded. People were bent over the sink. People were bent over in the bathroom. People rushed to the privy in the back yard and people dashed for the screen of blackberry bushes that lined the road.

Some of us were pale and some of us were red in the face. All of us were sweating profusely. Someone came in with a pitcher of creamy white liquid. "What's that?" asked Young Norman. "Plaster water, like Dr. Sather said to drink," was the answer.

"Don't drink it, don't drink it!" shouted Norman, "that's not lime, that's plaster of Paris!" (Sometimes, on warm evenings, I wonder just what would have happened if we'd all drunk plaster of Paris.)

The hubbub slowly sloughed off and we found ourselves sitting around listening to a deep silence punctuated by internal rumblings. And, suddenly, we all realized no one had died. Only Rock Freyer still was actually sick. Some of the men who had dashed in to help us bundled Rock up and took him to the hospital.

"I ate some poisoned clams," Rock told the doctor. But, after punching and probing and taking a blood count, the doctor said, "You didn't have any poisoned clams. What you've got is appendicitis. We'll get you into bed and get the thing out in the morning. You haven't taken any laxatives or anything like that, have you?"

"Well, now," Rock answered. "I had eight or nine glasses of hot salt water and some soda water—about six glasses. Then I drank some chittum bark in hot water and had a couple glasses of egg white. Only that and about three teaspoonsful of old H&H."

The young doctor looked at Rock for a long time. "Holy Christopher," said the doctor softly. He laid his fingers over Rock's appendix. "She's still there," he said, "but by all the rules she should have blown up long ago."

4

Strew Me the Ground with Daffodils

JUST ABOUT THE TIME Pappy's and Young Norman's new Levis had begun to fade, it occurred to all of us we should have some visible means of support. Norman had a part-time job driving a gravel truck along the beastly river road to Reedsport, and Pappy, now almost completely well, was nosing around the valley for something to do. I had appointed myself guardian of the dappled fawns. Two of the delicate creatures had adopted us (or our apple trees) and tripped into the yard every morning for breakfast. I was certain they would wander into the highway and be clobbered by a truck, so I stood guard and shooed them back from the highway every time they seemed inclined to commit suicide.

I was berating the fawns for their stupidity one morning when Young Norman sidled around the corner of the house (now painted a gleaming white). He ran his hand through his curly hair and then, very deliberately, lit his pipe. "What's the matter with you?" I asked. He was quiet for a long moment, drawing on the pipe, and then he said, "Aunt Gladys, either Pappy's a lot better or he's gone completely berserk. I'm not sure which." I waited. "He's just bought six tons of daffodils."

"Oh, Honey, you're kidding," I wailed. "We don't have half enough vases to hold that many flowers."

"Heck, I don't mean flowers," Young Norman said. "He's bought six tons of King Alfred daffodil bulbs. Ninety thousand of them. And he paid three thousand dollars for them."

"Ye Gods," I cried, "I better start looking up recipes for daffodils because it looks like that's what we're going to be eating."

"Now look, Mammy," said Young Norman. "We've got to be calm about this. Maybe if we just humor Pappy along, we can get the man to take them back." At that moment, Pappy stepped jauntily around the corner of the house and put us in place. His eyes were merry and he looked better than I had seen him in four years. He put his arm around me and smiled, "How does it feel to be the wife of a daffodil farmer?" he asked. He was so new at it, he didn't even know he was a "bulb grower," not a "daffodil farmer." I didn't say anything. "I've been talking to Paul Applegate and I think I know where we can get some land to lease," he prodded.

"Oh, Pappy," I moaned. "You don't even know which end of a bulb to stick in the ground. We don't even have a shovel to plant them with. We don't. . . ."

"Don't stand there telling me what we haven't got,"

Pappy said. "What we haven't got, I'll get. What we don't know, we can learn."

"All right," I said bleakly, "but you'd better start getting, and the first thing you better get is someone to tell you what to do. What do you think, Norman?" I asked.

Young Norman put on a quizzical expression. "I think we're in the daffodil business," he said. I was stunned and a little frightened. I had every faith in Pappy, but he'd never done anything remotely like farming—and now he had spent almost every cent we had on daffodils.

Pappy was so full of plans that evening that we all got a little enthusiastic, and wrote splendid figures on paper, contemplating a future golden with daffodils. "If everything goes right, we ought to harvest 90,000 blooms next spring," Pappy said. "Then we can sell our surplus bulbs and still have enough for next year."

That evening, too, he phoned an ad in to *The Port Umpqua Courier* ("Covers the Lower Umpqua Area Like the Dew"); "Man Wanted: Must be able to manage small daffodil acreage. Norman Workman, Scottsburg, Oregon." A few days later, Pappy had a letter from a man who sounded like exactly the person we needed. "I have been working in daffodils for the last eight years," it said. "I am familiar with field preparation, planting, picking and packing." It was signed, "V. Martin."

Pappy immediately wrote V. Martin, tentatively engaging his services, and the morning Martin was to arrive Pappy kept jumping up to look out the front window. Then he called, "Here he comes," and we all peered out and saw a pickup truck pulling up the steep slope from the road. All we could see on the front seat was a big yellow dog. "Holy Cow!" I said, "the dog's driving." Pappy went outside and we heard him booming, "That you, Martin? I'm glad to. . . ." His voice sort of trailed off and was lost in a babble of sound from the lips of a bitsy little woman who descended from the truck. Young Norman and I went out and Pappy introduced us. "My name is Val Martin," said the little lady. "You lak Mexicans, I'm Mexican. You lak Portuguese, I'm Portuguese. I don' care."

Val Martin weighed eighty-nine pounds. She wore a pair of Levis so tight they seemed painted on her tiny behind. Her black hair was covered with a red bandana handkerchief and she wore a plaid shirt. She had a delightful grin and her black eyes darted about, taking in everything there was to see. "Don' worry about nothin', my leetle peegeon," she said to me. "Val Martin knows everytheeng about daffodeels an' she's going to teach Pappy an' Stony wat they should do."

"Stony?" I inquired cautiously.

"Thees young one have the same name lak Stonewall Jackson. I theenk I call heem Stony. Okay?" We stood there for a moment with Val's yellow dog sniffing at us, and I wondered what was going through Pappy's mind. I could see him studying Val carefully, the five-foot-tall mite looking like a boiled-down pirate with her dark skin under the red bandana.

I don't remember ever really hiring Val formally, but she stayed with us ten years. She lived alone in a little house under the bridge at Elkton, eighteen miles east, and she knew everyone in the valley. People called her Pee-wee and no one ever used her last name. Young Norman and other men working in the fields would pick her up and play catch with her whenever they thought she was getting too bossy and Val would scream and laugh and cuss them. After she had been with us a time, I asked her to help me in the house. She did, but she was never happy about it. One day she said, "I mus' tol' you, my leetle pee-geon, I don' theenk I work for you any more." I was shocked. "Why, Val," I said. "What will we do? You know we can't get along without you."

"Oh, I'm not goin' to queet all of you," she said. "I theenk I work for Pappy and Stony. I don' theenk I lak to work for you."

"Is anything wrong?" I asked. "Did I do anything?"

"Oh, no," Val said, "but those damn fools make so many meestakes I worry all the time. I work in here but my heart ees out there." When she really quit after ten years, she said, "I theenk I don' come back any more." Then she laughed. "If you don' learn nothin' by now, I don' theenk you ever goin' to."

Under the dancing dark eye of Val Martin, Pappy and Stony tackled the art of daffodil farming. Pappy had leased a gently-sloping field just south of the river for his first year's crop and, with Val running alongside, Pappy and Stony learned to operate the tractor, learned how to plow, harrow and disc the furrows which were to receive the bulbs. Because of the slight slope, the tractor had a tendency to skid a bit, much to Val's displeasure. "Luke," she shouted at Pappy who was struggling to make a

73

straight, professional-looking furrow. "Luke at the track you leave. She luke lak she left by a snake weeth the belly-ache."

Eventually the field was ready for the bulbs. The furrows were primly aligned; bulb boxes were stacked precisely at the edge of the dentated field, the tractor retired to the sidelines. Val and Pappy and Stony were taking time for a smoke before plunging into the chore of planting, when they heard a motor boat chugging down the river. As they watched idly, the boat pulled around a bend and glided to the bank at the lower end of the field where there was a clump of myrtle. The boat was filled with women and children—who screamed up the bank the moment it touched shore. The ladies followed, carrying picnic baskets, collapsible chairs, artists' easels, and a folded camp stove.

"You tell them to go 'way, Pappy," said Val. "They breeng chairs an' beds an' a stove. Pretty soon, them damn women beeld a house an' you never get them out. You tell them to get the hell out now. Tell them we got to plant daffodeels."

"Now, Val," Pappy replied. "They won't hurt anything. We've got to remember the Good-Neighbor policy." One of the ladies, apparently the high priestess, approached Pappy. "This is such a lovely spot," she said, "we wondered if we could sketch a while and have our lunch here."

"Sure, go ahead," said Pappy, ignoring the black look he got from Val.

"Tell that damn lady to go 'way, Pappy," she muttered. The artist lady suddenly lit up like a juke box. "I've just

had the most marvelous idea," she shrilled. "Oh, if you'll
just say yes." Pappy waited. "I can see you are pioneer
stock," she gushed. "I'd so like to sketch you; the simple,
strong man of the soil, in this beautiful setting."

"Why, certainly," said Pappy. "I want to take a rest anyway." Pappy, who had jockeyed a desk for thirty years,
was tickled to be mistaken for a man of the soil. Making
little chittering noises, the lady dashed off to get her
sketching equipment and Pappy, solemnly puffing his
pipe, patiently posed. "Yah," Val yelled. "Now she has you
seeting lak a dog. Pretty soon she make you point at the
birds." She and Stony went to work, on their hands and
knees, plunking the daffodil bulbs into the furrows. From
time to time, Val returned to the artist to give critical attention. "Oh, wat a terrible peecture," she said. "Why don'
you make it a leetle darker here an' a leetle not so dark
over here? Ho, Pappy, she make you luke lak Charlie
Chapleen."

"I'll have you know I've painted and sketched for
twenty years," sniffed the artist.

"I don' geev a damn how long you paint," sneered Val.
"You don' know how to make Pappy luke lak Pappy."

Val went back to her chore. The pastoral scene was
drowsily complete: Val and Stony stooping at their work,
kingfishers darting in and out of the trees, a cluster of
women sketching the lazy Umpqua under the sky, the
rumble of a log truck far away, and, over all, the good
smell of newly-turned earth.

Then, without warning, the tractor starter whined, the
engine coughed a couple of times and then roared to life.
The noise was extraordinary. With a mighty lunge, the

tractor took off over the field. Children screamed triumphantly. Pappy, the simple soilsman, blasted off the simple soil like a Polaris missile, clutching the air as he rose. Stony dropped his pipe and loped toward the tractor but, in the rough field, he did not have a chance of catching it.

A red-haired girl, about eleven, was in the driver's seat, clutching the steering wheel. She had a look of radiant, desperate jubilation on her white face and her little fanny banged against the bucket seat as the tractor rolled and pitched and macerated the prim furrows. Three boys chased the girl, shouting, "Get off! It's our turn now."

Val's black eyes darted fire. She stood with her legs spread and cursed. "Oh, you damn fool keed," she screamed. "Stupeed, stupeed keed." The lady artist departed in a shower of charcoal dust and sketching paper and took off after her daughter on the tractor. "Stop her!" she cried. "Oh, my poor baby. She'll be killed."

She wasn't just whistling Dixie, either. There was every good chance the child could hurt herself badly. Norman and Pappy stood appalled. Val kept up a running commentary on the child, her mother and other relatives. The mother, still stumbling over the furrows, shouted, "Stop her! Somebody stop her or I'll sue you. I'll sue." The red-haired driver, her freckles stark against her white skin, was enjoying every minute of her perilous ride. She looked over her shoulder to taunt the boys and turned the wheel just enough so the tractor smashed head on into a stack of bulb boxes. Bulbs and boxes flew in all directions but the tractor sailed on.

"Stop! It's our turn now," shouted the boys.

"Stop! I'll sue," shrieked the mother.

"That keed's goin' to keel herself," shouted Val.

Completely out of control, the tractor swerved to the edge of the field, turned toward the river, hiccuped through a small ditch and rammed solidly against a myrtle tree. The engine died. There was a sudden quiet in which the redhead turned and smiled at the boys. "Okay," she said. "It's your turn now." Her smile lasted approximately three seconds. Her mother snatched her off the tractor and dragged her toward the boat. Other mothers grabbed the boys and hustled them toward the river. In a few minutes, collapsible lady artists, collapsible chairs and stoves, easels and children were out of sight.

"Peekneekers," sneered Val, looking at the lacerations in her precise daffodil field, the scattered boxes and the scarred tractor. She turned to Pappy with great scorn. "Gude neighbor poleecee, hey? Luke, Pappy, nex' time some damn fool peekneekers come here, you tell them to go *up* the reever, go *don* the reever, go to *hell*, go *any place* but don' stay here!"

One person who became a great favorite with Val was my mother. She had come to stay with us while the daffodils were bedded down for the winter. "I theenk a nice ol' fat lady lak you should have a husban'," Val told her. (My father had died in 1938.)

"Who've you got in mind?" laughed Mama.

"Oh, I don' have nobody yet," said Val, "but I luke aroun'. I fin' somebody, you see." Every few days, she nominated a candidate.

"I fin' a nice man for you in the Bomb Shelter, that tavern in Elkton," she announced, giggling, "but I don'

77

theenk you goin' to like heem because he dreenks all the time an' won' work." Old Abe turned out to be her prize. "I theenk maybe you should take thees ol' guy," Val said, "because he's got a couple of goats and you can go into the cheese business."

"Sounds pretty good," said Mama. "Has he got a nice house?"

"Oh, it must be a nice house, all right," Val said. "These goats leeve right een there weeth him an' *they* lak it. I tol' heem he should come and see you."

Old Abe came the next day. He is a typical hermit, loves all animals, and proves it by sharing his small mountain cabin with his chickens, two turkeys, ducks, civet cats which come daily, and his goats. He's worked out a fairly complex *simple* life which suits him well. Abe lives about three miles up a canyon on the south side of the river. When he ventures into the valley, which he does often, he hikes down the mountain and, in summer, clambers across the "summer" bridge which the log trucks use. Then he picks up a bicycle he hides in a special place and pedals the six miles into Scottsburg, greeting everyone cheerily and stopping to do odd jobs. He'll do almost anything: he'll trap a beaver, mend a fence, run an errand or work in the fields or gardens. In the winter, when the summer bridge is under water, he rows over to pick up his bike.

Mama took one look at Old Abe as he stood at the back door and dashed into the house. "Wait'll I get hold of that Val," she said. Old Abe raised his hat politely and this gallant gesture allowed a few of his spiky, sticky yellow hairs to escape the plastered-down mass on the top of his head. He wore an old Army overcoat handed down by Colonel Rex Applegate, Paul's son, who weighs about 225 pounds. Since Old Abe pushes the scales at 160, the coat draped around him like a toga. His shoes, also Army issue, were presentable but his trousers carried the droppage of a hundred bachelor meals, egg spots, splotches of meat juice, souring milk, jam, and a dozen unidentifiable stains.

"Wup, wup, wup," he said, his weather-beaten face serious. "Beautiful day. Beautiful day." (It was, in fact, raining very hard.) "Wup, wup, Peewee told me to stop in. Said you might have a job I could do." I asked him in and he said, "Well, sure. Well, sure." We invited him in to have cake and coffee. As we talked, about all we could make out of his part of the conversation was, "Oom-hoom, oom-hoom," with an occasional "Wup." He did manage to tell us that he was thinking of getting a radio: "Mighty lonesome up there with those damn goats all the time and no news." When he was leaving I offered him some jam. "Wup, I love home-made jam. Right nice of you. Wup. Right nice." He stepped into the rain and sloshed away on his bike, just as our phone rang. "Heard Old Abe was at your place," said Paul Applegate. "You be sure and let me know when he leaves. Got to catch him today and see that he takes a bath and then I've got to make him sit still long enough for someone to take a scythe to that crop of hair."

Since then Old Abe has dropped around about once a week for a visit. He doesn't read or write but that has never bothered him and he is surprisingly well-informed. He's a very good listener, and right there is an accomplishment rare enough.

79

Pappy fairly dived into the daffodil business. He got books from the State University and the Department of Agriculture and he pored over them every night. Pappy (as I could have predicted) was wrestling with farming just as he had wrestled and mastered everything else he'd faced in life. At the drop of a voice, he could give you endlessly fascinating (or anyway, endless) facts and figures about the daffodil bulb, the narcissus fly (its only foe), the use of cyanide against this marauder, methyl bromide, the newest weapon against fly and offspring, pre-cooling of buds, and just about anything else you'd care to know about daffodils.

Once the bulbs were in the ground, there was nothing to do but wait until they bloomed. This would happen in mid-February. Meanwhile, I continued to lose every round in my passive war against the ways of the valley. The word was now being circulated that I was too stuck up to help Pappy and Norman in the field. But the hardest blow came one bitter day in Reedsport, the little village which makes the Umpqua melancholy as it nears the ocean. I had driven down on the spur of the moment and it wasn't until I was in Reedsport that I realized I faced a dilemma: I had left my purse, containing all my money and gasoline credit cards at home; I had no money and no gasoline. I rummaged around in the glove compartment of the car and found a checkbook, however, so I started about my errands without a care. Without a care, that is, until I offered a check for groceries. "I'm sorry," said the girl at the check stand, "but I think you'd better see the manager about that check." The manager was very embarrassed but he made it clear he did not want my paper.

"Why don't you ask Mr. Burdick at the drug store to cash it?" he suggested. "Then you can pay me."

"You mean you won't take my check?" I asked.

"That's what I mean," he said.

Well, nothing like that had ever happened to me before and I was irritated, insulted, indignant, angry, outraged and downright stomping mad, in the order named, as I went across the street to the drug store. Mr. Burdick was kind. "I'll be glad to lend you some money, Mrs. Workman," he said, "but I'd rather not take that check."

"But why not?" A tremendous effort of will enabled me to keep my voice down to a shout.

"Well, I'd just rather not, that's all," replied the druggist, looking at his feet. I now became incensed, infuriated and infantile.

"I'll walk home first," I shrilled, flouncing out of the store. I stood on a corner in a cold, drizzly rain, in the slush of a recent snow and bawled, I was so mad. "What in the devil is this all about?" I thought. "We're not as bad as all that! Sure, maybe they don't want us socially, maybe they think I don't get up 'til noon, maybe I don't work in the fields, but for gosh sakes, our money ought to be all right." Then I thought, "We'll just get out of here and go back to California." And then I thought of the $3000 Pappy had planted in the ground and I bawled some more.

At home, Pappy and Norman were worrying. When it got dark and they had not heard from me, they were sure I had gone off the twisty river road. Driving slowly to spot any place a car might have left the road, they went to Reedsport and found me standing on frozen feet. I did

81

not even say "thanks" for my rescue. "We're going to sell all those bulbs and we're going to get out of here," I muttered. "I hate this valley and I hate everyone in it."

Pappy, as usual, was calm. "You're just getting upset; you'll land in the hospital if this keeps up."

Pappy was right. I made the room with the white side walls the next day with my nerves doing nip-ups and my heart pounding. Later, Pappy nosed around to see who had scuttled our credit. He found a banker in his cups had passed the word we did not have enough money to cover purchase of the bulbs. (Pappy had given a deposit and had sent to Los Angeles for savings to cover the balance.) Many high words were spoken and the whole mess was straightened out eventually, but it was another black mark against me.

In October, the silverside salmon nosed up the river from the ocean and Pappy and Norman were out almost every day, either right in front of the house or at Sawyer's Rapids, a few miles up the river. Day after day they brought in gleaming fish. In November and December the steelhead fought the rapids. In weather so cold I hugged the stove, Pappy and Norman and Paul Applegate rigged a canvas shelter for protection against the rain and wind, built a fire, and sat blissfully for hours, waiting for a steelhead to call. "I may be the one they call nuts around here," I said, "but I'm not crazy enough to fish in this weather." Pappy grinned. "It's a bad disease," he said, "and when it gets to you, nothing can save you. Except maybe some more steelhead fishing." Pappy and Norman both got their bucks, someone gave us a quarter of elk, and the freezer was brimming with wonderful provender, including flat pans filled with ice—covering dozens of tiny brook trout.

Now all was gray on the Umpqua, gray clouds, gray river, gray mornings, gray rain. Drivers of the big trucks who dripped in for coffee left muddy tracks behind them. The cats huddled morosely on the back porch, infrequently picking their way between the puddles outside. Something of the grayness of the valley seemed plunged deep inside me. I was gray. I'd sleep eleven hours a night and get up too groggy to navigate. After lunch, I'd take a nap—actually, it was not so much taking a nap as simply falling asleep wherever I happened to sit. I drank gallons of coffee and still I slept. Once, at Jane and Ken Murphy's house, I dozed off right in the middle of dinner. I began spending more time in Yoncalla, but nothing could satisfy my body's craving for sleep. Pappy and I realized something new was wrong with me but the doctors were just as puzzled as we.

So the long, gray, dripping, featureless winter passed. Just as Pappy was girding for his first picking season—the season on which our whole financial future hinged—it began to snow. It snows rarely in the valley, but now the white fluffed from the somber skies for two days and the thermometer dropped alarmingly. I went with Pappy to look at the daffodil field across the river. It was a desolate drive, west to Scottsburg, across the bridge to the south bank, then east for four or five miles on the slippery logging road. And when we came to our field, my heart almost broke at the look on Pappy's face. The snow had erased the furrows. And, in the freezing weather, the daffodils had just given up. The long leaves lay like green straps, flat on the snow. The buds were prostrate, too. It was clear as anything could be that Pappy's first daffodil crop was doomed.

But Val Martin came by that evening. "Don' worry, I tol' you," she said. "Those daffodeels are okay. It don' make no deeference to them eef eet snows. I tol' you, when the sun comes out a leetle, everytheeng is goin' to be okay." Pappy just stared at Val; what kind of nonsense was she talking? Hadn't he seen the daffodils, lying like lifeless things in the snow? And yet, the miracle happened. With all the hushed drama of a resurrection, the daffodils raised their leaves and yellowing buds a few hours after a warm rain and watery sunshine filled the field.

Just before picking time, I was in Yoncalla for another bout of sleeping, but Maude Applegate jerked me back. "Gladys simply has to pull herself together and cook for the pickers," she told Pappy. "All the growers have a good hot lunch for their people and, if you don't, you'll soon lose your pickers." So I went back to the valley.

Picking time is the most exciting in the year. Then come the people from all over the valley, ready for their assault on the buds, which must be picked before they open. Most of the pickers were local women, with a sprinkling of men and a few school boys. All of them seemed grotesquely fat. "Don' you worry about eet, my leetle peegeon," said Val. "When the sun comes up, you watch and see. Those peekers get thinner then." As usual, Val knew. As the day warmed up, the pickers began to shed layer after layer of outer clothes, and by noon all of them looked normal.

Watching the pickers fascinated me. They wear rubber gloves to protect their hands against the acid juice of the daffodil stalk. Working stooped over and very fast, they run their right hand down the bud stalk, grasping it between thumb and forefinger. Then, with a quick snap, they break the stem as cleanly as though it were cut with a knife. Pickers do not talk as they work. Their minds are entirely taken up with counting to twenty-five, the number of buds in a bunch. When they gather a bunch, they snap a rubber band around the stems, stick the bunch under their left arm, and start again. After a few days, the pickers suffer a unique occupational disease: they can't stop counting to twenty-five. They count the number of times they chew, the houses on the way home, stars, trees, cars—always in groups of twenty-five. Twenty-five birds; twenty-five rocks; twenty-five . . .

I still had a terrible case of sleepiness. In the midst of cooking one day, I realized I could not keep my eyes open a moment longer. With a tremendous effort, I managed to turn off the burners under everything on the stove. At least, I thought I had. Then I fell into oblivion on the bed. When Pappy and the pickers came in for lunch, they thought the house was on fire. The vegetables had burned to blackness and were sending off long smudges of smoke. The meat, which I had managed to turn off, was half done. That ended my cooking.

"Mrs. Workman is too sick to cook," Pappy told the pickers. "You can bring your own lunches and she'll provide

coffee or you can buy your lunches and I'll pay for them."
The pickers began bringing lunches from home. And
when other growers heard we no longer furnished lunch,
their wives stopped cooking, too. That was just the first of
several revolutionary changes Pappy brought about in
the daffodil business in the valley.

The word that I was fiddling while lunch burned got
around the valley in four seconds flat, confirming once
and for all the fact I was dangerously mad. Would a sane
woman calmly lie down and go to sleep while food was on
the fire? *She would not!* Pappy came in for a lot of sympathy: that nice man, tied to a woman whose mind was so
far out she was hardly ever conscious. None of this bothered me. I slept eighteen to twenty hours a day and my
waking hours were blurred. I lost thirty pounds in this
do-it-yourself Nirvana. Whenever I realized how slim I
was, I was cheered in a sleepy sort of way.

When the picking season was over, Pappy made me his
first order of business. Whenever I felt up to it, he'd pack
me in the car and set out—usually for Portland, 185 miles
away—for a new doctor or another consultation of spe-
cialists. Finally, my ailment was diagnosed. I was suffering from something called narcolepsy, a form of sleeping
sickness caused by lack of adrenal cortex hormone. A few
shots of the proper hormone woke me up—and I've been
awake ever since, thanks to the shots and, more recently,
pills.

Pappy and Norman took off nearly 90,000 daffodil buds that first year and, glory be, the market was good.
When the bulbs were dug in the summer, the original
six tons had increased to ten tons and Pappy sold his

surplus to a flower house in Chicago. We were in the daffodil business and prospering.

Sad to say, however, my personal tonnage also increased mightily. No sooner had the sleeping sickness been arrested than I regained the thirty lost pounds. In a matter of seconds.

❀ ❀ *5* ❀ ❀

Wake Up, Old Lady, We're Almost Drowned

ALL BIG CITIES, I suppose, have their share of violence and social upheaval. But back in Los Angeles it had never seemed that way. The passions, storms, crimes, and lust all seemed sopped up by the crowd. I'd read in the newspapers about shootings and sluggings, about movie starlets flipping from bed to bed, about anonymous figures flinging themselves from office windows, but the reality always foundered somewhere in the gray prose. None of it touched me. Fires routed scores in scanty nightdress, but always on the other side of town; automobiles crashed with a sort of rhythmic regularity, but never in my vicinity. Floods meant only that the gutters filled with water for a few hours.

On the Umpqua, there is no crowd to blot up reality. If a house burns, it belongs to someone you know. A mud slide affects you and everyone around you. You do not read about it in the newspaper; you see it happen or you hear it fresh and hot. All this came to me gradually, and soon I realized violence was bubbling and churning just under the surface of the placid valley, ready to explode from second to second. Evidence was everywhere. The white and naked tree trunks picketing the hilltops like columns of some ruined temple: a reminder of the fires which ravaged the woods. Rows and rows of squat white stumps where the lumbermen had passed, like tombstones in the green of the second growth. Something sinister in the sound of a dynamite blast tumbling through the forest, some foreboding in the rumble of the huge trucks slamming down the treacherous forest roads. The first time I went to Scottsburg, I saw one man with no left arm, one man with no left hand, another so stooped and bent he could scarcely walk, and a fourth with a hook curling out from his sleeve end. Loggers, I was told, wearing the badges of their trade.

Violence was constant but was not obtrusive. The valley people had lived with it a long time and they actually enjoyed it, I believe; valley excitements were almost always violent. In a way, this helped explain Emma Hedden for me. One minute, Emma is so mild she practically evaporates. The next minute she'll tear like a buzz saw and use some pretty choice loggers' language. They told me about Emma and Blacky.

Blacky was the biggest man ever seen in the valley, stacking up near six feet six and weighing close to 300 pounds. He was fantastically strong. Blacky was a high climber and, with all his strength, was the gentlest fellow in the woods. He always took a dozen sandwiches into the forest for lunch, and sometimes a couple of pies, but he did not eat all that. He'd wander away from the rest of the crew and seek out birds and squirrels and he would eat with them. Gentle Blacky, like an over-size St. Francis, would sit on a log and open his lunch pail to the whole forest. Deer and skunks—and not any of your de-odorized skunks, either—squirrels and jays, would settle down for the meal, picking daintily at the morsels Blacky offered. Even the humming birds ate out of Blacky's hands.

This lovable, gentle giant was not above having an *apéritif* before dinner, maybe a dozen or so, and since his *apéritifs* were straight whiskey, he frequently got very drunk. When he was drunk, he was terrible to behold because then he loved people even more than he loved animals. He always wanted to dance with someone and, since there were no women at the logging camp across the river from Emma Hedden's store, he'd insist on dancing with the men. No one liked to refuse because Blacky was strong enough to tear ordinary loggers in two, but nobody wanted to dance with him, either, because he'd grab them so tight he'd break their ribs.

His last memorable drunk went according to pattern. He drank and he sang. "Will there be any jools, any jools in your crown—when at ev'ning the sun goeth down?" he roared. He went through "Onward Christian Soldiers," "Bringing in the Sheaves," and his favorite, "While the Lamp Holds Out to Burn, the Vilest Sinner May Return." As his hideous voice called hymns down the river, people nodded; "Blacky's packing a load tonight, for sure." Then Blacky wanted to dance, but he could not find a partner. He went from room to room in the bunk-house and turned over the beds, looking for his friends. In the last room, he came upon three loggers standing nervously in the far corner. One of them held his rifle like a club, but was afraid to smack Blacky with it. With a sunny smile, Blacky grabbed two of the men. "Let's dance," he bellowed happily. The logger waggled his rifle. "You come near me, you big ape, and I'll let you have this," he said. "Why, boys," Blacky roared. "I don't want to hurt you. The Bible says, 'Love your brothers,' and that's what I do. But, if you won't dance, then by God, I'm going to throw you in the river." And he did. One at a time, he looped his brothers through the window and into the placid Umpqua.

Then he wandered outside and saw the garbage cans. He grabbed one loaded can and whirled with it, spraying garbage all over the place. He picked up another and whirled again. "Let's just shoot him," one of the loggers said darkly, "before he kills us all." Before this suggestion could be acted on, a jeep slid to a stop and Emma Hedden got out. Blacky was now lying happily in a pile of garbage. Emma, all five feet four of her, plumped her way over to him. "Look, you big hulk of a woodenheaded ox," she said. "You get up and clean up this mess or I'll kick every tooth out of your stupid head." For emphasis, she hauled off and kicked him as hard as she could, on the shoulder. ("I wouldn't have kicked his teeth out," she explained later. "I just wanted to scare him.") Blacky staggered to his feet. As his face came within range, Emma belted him with the flat of her hand. "Now clean up this junk," she said.

"Aw, now, Miss Hedden," Blacky whimpered. "I ain't had my supper and this mess'll turn my stomach." "Clean it up NOW," shouted Emma, and marched into the dining hall for coffee. The other loggers, laughing now that Blacky was tamed, were eating supper. There was a slight commotion and Emma noticed Blacky, trying to compress his bulk into invisibility, crawling toward his place at the table. Emma let him crawl all the way to his chair. Then she kicked him hard enough on his broad behind to rearrange his brains. "Where'd you think you're going?" she snarled. "Get back out there and clean up that garbage." Blacky whined, "I'm hungry, Miss Hedden." But Emma was implacable. She reared back her foot for another kick and Blacky started to get up from his hands and knees. "The hell you do," cried Emma. "Crawl out the way you come in." Poor old Blacky crawled out.

I'd look at Emma in her store, with her steel-colored hair wrapped around her head in a single braid, dabs of rouge on her cheeks, reading a letter for a man who couldn't read for himself, or helping someone send off a letter to the mail order house (and probably lending him the money), and it was hard to see her in the role of giant killer. Now I know Emma Hedden is one of the strongest women ever fabricated. I have no doubt that Emma Hedden could run General Motors if she put her mind to it, and it's probably a good thing for the Ford Company that she prefers to run her little store in Scottsburg.

Of all the forms of violence that could erupt in the valley the two most feared are fire and flood. During our time we have seen both. *The* Umpqua Valley flood was in 1861; *our* flood is always referred to as a "freshet." After going through the Freshet, I'm perfectly content that I was not present for the Flood.

The first rains of the season were usual: little try-out rains that soaked into the ground immediately, washed off the foliage of the firs, sluiced the dust from the gold and scarlet leaves and made the valley look radiant again after the slow summer. The tall sky was filled with galleon clouds that sailed majestically overhead in the changing light of the day and threw down cottony reflections on the slow-moving Umpqua.

These clouds soon loosed a torrential downpour that made the creeks and rivulets boil through the forest and stippled the surface of the wind-driven river. For a few days there was a calm, and then, in the night, the gentle, plodding, business-like, down-to-earth Oregon rain we know so well began. Hour after hour the skies dripped and the thirsty fields and forests soaked up the moisture. Day after day the sky continued its steady, everlasting weeping and the earth had sponged up all the water it could hold. Water oozed and then began to pour from the highway cuts. Sloping fields lunged gently down hill. The Umpqua silently began to rise in its summer bed, covered the water weeds, and began to inch toward the willows. The dripping from the eaves became a constant and the gurgle of water in the drainspouts was our melody day and night. The forest roads were impassable.

Shortly before Christmas, after weeks of the insistent, incessant rains, a hill near Reedsport inched its way toward the highway and then, with a crashing of trees and a slushy sliding of rock and mud, gave up being a hill and collapsed in a muddy avalanche across the highway and into the river, blocking access to the coastal area. We heard of several people who had been caught on the "wrong" side of the slide in Reedsport. Loggers rolled out their bulldozers and pushed ineffectually at the mud; as soon as a bladeful of muck had been cleared from the road, the slide oozed a few feet farther and no mark remained of the clean-up effort. A few nights later, Dorothy and Walter Palmer had just arrived at their home on Paradise Creek and heard their phone ringing over and over. Dorothy answered. "Are you all right?" asked a frightened voice.

"I guess so," answered Dorothy. "Why? Is something supposed to be the matter with me?"

"Thank God you're safe. This is Sue Smith at Sawyer's Rapids and we saw you go by here a few minutes ago. And just the minute you passed, it seemed to us, Slidden Out Gulch went out. The whole hill slid right onto the road, all the big trees and everything and we thought sure you people were caught in it."

Now the narrow valley was plugged effectively at both ends by head-high barriers of mud and twisted trees and rocks. "This is not going to be much of a Christmas," the valley people said: many of them had ordered their Christmas presents from mail order houses and they knew they would never be delivered on time. Emma Hedden began rationing flour and sugar for Christmas cookies and cakes, allocating the larger portions to families with the most children. The last of the store bread left Emma's shelves, and valley women warmed their ovens for a stint of home baking.

Incredible as it seemed, a few people were able to traverse the mud barriers. Roy Chenoweth, whose dairy near Reedsport supplied most of the milk to the valley, somehow made his way through the mud and mire every day. "Not one of my babies missed a single delivery of milk," he says with a pride we all share. Roy waded, shoved and augered his body through the waist-high, shoulder-high mud with a rope hooked onto him from a caterpillar which half dragged him through the slimy mass. "It was sort of like water skiing," Roy laughs, "only I didn't have any skis and the water was pretty solid."

And still it rained. Under the unremitting showers, the Umpqua, which had been swelling slowly, began to bulge and pick up speed. The water became brown with mud and its surface was churned with angry lashings as it sucked higher and higher on its banks. The berserk stream growled and snarled and clawed through the willows and brambles. Its heavy, heaving surface tumbled chicken coops, privies, and overturned boats. Hundreds of logs shot by, now and again leaping out of the water and falling back with great geysers of muddy water. Whole trees, their roots looming out of the water like high poop decks of ships, swirled toward the ocean. The raging river tore into unprotected banks, chewing off jutting points to widen its bed. Foot by racing foot, the Umpqua rose; it spread from its usual banks to become a torrent almost a quarter of a mile wide.

The party line stuttered, faltered and finally succumbed some time during this hectic day and, just at dusk, the electricity went out, too. Our house and most of the other, older houses were built high above the stream, but we knew of others that must be feeling the shuddering blows of the river. Just before dark, Young Norman splashed through the rain to warn a couple, new to the valley, that their house (which had been flooded in other years when the river was comparatively mild) was almost certain to be inundated. He found them staring uncomprehendingly at the boisterous river racing by almost at the foundation of their house. "The river looks pretty bad," he said. "If I were you I sure would get out now." The man took a gulp of whiskey from a glass as he watched the river. He turned as though he had not heard and pulled at the whiskey again. "I don't think she's coming up any more," he said. "I've been watching. Hell, it'd have to have twice as much water as it's got now to get 'way up here, and nobody'll make me believe that's going to happen."

Norman departed but he fretted all evening as he watched the river rising steadily and heard it roaring in the night. Finally, he could stand it no longer. He grabbed up a flashlight and ran through the storm to the house. He was brought up short by the river, which churned around the house at window level. He shouted but got no answer so he waded into the stream and into the house. He flashed his light across the flooded room. Stove wood floated in lazy swirls, a table was afloat. And then he saw a tiny baby asleep on an air mattress which floated gently above the stove!

Norman pelted up the stairs and found the man and woman peacefully asleep. He routed them out and got them to Scottsburg where Emma took them into her big

97

house. They were not the only refugees there; Emma's house was overflowing with families that had been flooded out. "They just keep coming," she said to Norman. "I haven't any idea how many I've got now." A banging on the front door interrupted her. "Here come some more, I'll bet," she said. But she was wrong. It was time for her to drop her role as ministering angel and go into her act as community cop.

"There's a bunch of loggers playing poker and drinking in a shack down by the river and they won't move," she said. "I guess I've got to go down and drill some sense into their fool heads before they all drown." She put on a raincoat and trudged out into the dripping night. She was walking in water before she reached the shack and the river was lapping over the threshold and washing around the feet of the poker players. Emma stood in the doorway; five loggers and a couple of women were seated at a kitchen table by the light of a kerosene lamp. A bottle of whiskey held the place of honor in the middle of the table. "Hey, you guys," Emma said quietly. "Don't you have the sense God gave you? Get out of here before the place washes down the river."

"Don't get yourself all excited, Emma," said the host. "I got the damnedest winning streak I've ever had and I ain't going to quit now for nothing or nobody." He regarded Emma owlishly in the gloom of the lamp and suddenly reached up and tried to switch on the light which hung over the table.

"Don't do that!" Emma shouted. "If the electricity comes on you'll be electrocuted." His wife joined in. "Aw, the electricity's not going to come on 'til next summer," she said. "What we need is some more kerosene. Get us some, will you, Emma?" Emma stomped out.

She couldn't forget the drunks, however, and a few hours later she went back to the shack, wading knee deep in the muddy water. The poker players were bleary-eyed by now, and looked up sluggishly when Emma opened the door. The water was up to the level of their chairs and still they played on. "All right," Emma said, "get out of here right now. If you don't move, I'm going to get some guys in here after you and they'll be guys big enough to make you move."

"I'm going," said one of the players. "It ain't no use staying in here. I can't win nothing anyway and I'm tired of sitting with my hind end in cold water."

"Me, too," said another. "I'm out eighty bucks and my boots are full of mud." The loggers sloshed out of the room.

"I win so much money I don't care what happens now," said the host unsteadily. "Come on in, Emma, and have a drink. We'll do a sailor's hornpipe before the damned ol' ship sinks." He opened the door on the river side and the stream gushed in. "Ship ahoy!" he hollered. He shoved the poker table out through the door and watched it float away. He threw a chair out the door. "Let 'er go," giggled his wife. "We don't want the old stuff anyways." Piece by piece he sent every bit of furniture out into the flood. "Women and children first," he yelled, "and I go down with the ship." He turned to Emma. "Get outa here, lady. We want to get some sleep." He and his wife waded over

99

to the bed—the mattress was about four inches above the water—and flopped down heavily. "G'night, Emma," the logger said thickly. "Take to the boats. The stinkin' ol' ship's goin' down."

Emma went over to the shack the next morning when the water had receded a bit. The logger and his wife were still asleep. "I thought they were both dead," Emma said. She shook them awake. The logger looked at the mud on the floor in the empty room. He looked at the river raging by a few feet from his door. "Wake up, old lady," he said to his wife. "There's a hell of a big flood and we're almost drowned."

"They didn't even catch a bad cold," Emma sniffed.

As long as the river was on its bender, the valley remained effectively stoppered. (It was some bender: the Umpqua rose forty-three feet; we know because our house, forty-five feet above the river, just missed getting wet.) But the river finally sobered up. The Umpqua Navigation Co. put on a small boat to traverse the river from Reedsport to Scottsburg and communications of a sort were established. The valley was completely closed for ten days, and for thirteen weeks most communications were jumbled, with no regular deliveries of food and produce.

With the road blocked, Scottsburg children could not get to school in Reedsport by school bus and they basked in the prospect of a long vacation. They should have known better. School officials arranged with the railroad to run a special school train over the logging tracks and every day the kids rode in style. Most of the children had never ridden in a train before. One of the boys, overwhelmed by the magnificence of the train, described its superior features at great length. Then he turned to me, "Maybe you won't believe this, but there's a privy in every car."

6

On Flora, On Ceres, Come On, Pomona

S PRING in the Umpqua Valley makes all the winter rain seem worth while. The valley, which masquerades during the interminable gray months as a sullen, pinch-mouthed, teary-eyed spinster, suddenly feels her juices and begins to dance about in a flagrantly wanton way. Umpqua spring is a rollicking virginal maid, but she gives you the feeling she won't be that way long unless she shows a *little* restraint.

Acres of Scotch broom, which hide under a respectable green most of the year, shake out banners of magnificent golden bloom. Drone bees start warm-up flights for the annual game of "Who Gets the Queen." Sammy the cat, always ready, is readier. Beavers and otter, which hid out all winter in their secret places, go about their chores with a certain look in their eyes. The sky is full of wild drakes chasing their dowdy females toward the mating season as fast as wings can flap. Hundreds of wild apple trees announce the season in subtle white and pink finery. Digitalis sends up its spires of azure; lilac lights up the dark places and fills the air with a heady sweetness. Trillium, wild iris and columbines, and even the clumsy crawler known as "old-man-in-the-ground" put on their sexiest blossoms, gaudy signs that pollen is available. Pink and white dogwoods blaze in the shadows and rhododendron —fifteen feet high—and azalea make the forest a surprise and delight with their shouting pink blooms.

Did we join this heady dance? Well, in a manner of speaking, we did. We joined the Grange. It was a happy moment for me because the invitation to join meant I was accepted by the community. I had the feeling a few eyebrows might still have been trying to set altitude records whenever my name was mentioned, but I grabbed at the Grange accolade gratefully and happily.

The Grange is a secret organization, a lodge, a unit of the "Patrons of Husbandry" open to both men and women of agriculture. It is dedicated to the education and elevation of the American farmer, leans heavily on such Roman deities as Ceres, goddess of the harvest, Flora, goddess of flowers, and Pomona, goddess of fruit. It abounds with outer and inner guards, chaplains, masters and ritual. Everything starts and ends with a prayer (not to the Roman gods).

In the valley, the Grange is the pivot on which everything turns: the forum for kneading local problems, the platform for ideas, both good and bad, the setting for the valley's exquisitely amateur theater, the scene of gargantuan feasts, a boundless source of charity-starts-at-home good works. The hall is used for Grange meetings, socials, political rallies, dances and funerals. In a word, the Grange is the heart and soul—and muscle—of the valley. Almost everyone belongs, and even those who do not can participate in many of its public galas.

Laughter was one of the mainstays of our Grange. I always liked to see Tiny Justesen at the Grange feeds because she made everyone laugh just to be near her. Tiny is an enormous bundle of lady who rolls from side to side when she walks. "I weighed her once," Emma Hedden said. "Weighed 405 pounds."

"You think she'd weigh that much on anybody else's scales?" Pappy asked dryly.

"You think I'm fat?" Tiny giggles. "I swear before God I'm the smallest one in my family. Everybody around me is big except my man. He only weighs 106." And Tiny bellows with laughter and everyone around laughs, too. Whenever Grandma Butler bakes apple custard pie for a Grange food sale, she always bakes at least two because she knows Tiny will want one. Tiny scrapes through the door sideways, her eyes fixed on the food tables, and always hollers, "Is Grandma Butler here? If she is, I got hosies on one of them apple custard pies." I couldn't make out what she meant by "hosies" until I saw her buy and eat a whole pie. I think she is saying "wholesies" which means she gets the whole shebang, because if there is one piece out of a pie, Tiny doesn't want it. (Old Abe always looks dark when Tiny arrives. Since he always gets to take the leftovers home, he regards Tiny as a natural enemy.) "You just got to tell me how you make that pie," Tiny bellowed at Grandma Butler one evening. "That's the finest thing I've ever seen."

105

"You ready?" asked Grandma Butler. "Get a pencil and I'll try to remember everything that goes in. First you take a pint of stewed apples, and an egg, a large lump of butter, a cup and a half of sugar, a half cup of cream, a heaping teaspoonful of flour and a little salt. You can put in some cinnamon and things like that, too. Then beat it all together and bake it in an unbaked pie crust, just like you make a custard pie, and that's all there is to it."

Some deep, delightful instinct, some great magic enters into the cooking of the Umpqua Valley. The valley women can take a prosaic item like fried chicken and create a mouth-watering delight of such succulent goodness that every chicken that ever lived is thereby glorified. I asked Mrs. Houser, from up Smith River, just how she manages to make her fried chicken taste so heavenly and this is what she wrote: "Take a chicken. I would druther have a rooster. I would druther have the rooster about four pounds. Kill it. Scald it. Pick it. Draw it. Wash it plenty. Now cut it up. Salt it and let it stand over night. Don't let the flies get on it. Flour it good and fry it in good, fresh, hot lard. Make some good brown chicken gravy and don't be afraid to use some cream in the gravy. That's how I cook fried chicken." If Southerners ever discover how to fry chicken as well as Mrs. Houser, they'll secede again —in their pride.

Even I have become a pretty good cook, mostly by cadging recipes from the good ladies of the Grange. My greatest success has been scored with a barbecue sauce so versatile it can be used (with taste-tingling wonder) with beans, salmon, elk, venison and meat balls. Emma Hedden says the recipe has been a favorite so long and has been improved so many times it is impossible to credit its discovery to any single person: the barbecue sauce is a triumph of the valley. Here it is:

Cook slowly two cups of onions and one cup of celery (both finely diced) in four tablespoons of bacon fryings (do not brown). Then add three small cans of tomato sauce, three-fourths cup of molasses (not Karo), one cup of brown sugar (packed down in the cup), one-half cup vinegar, three-fourths cup catsup, two tablespoons Worcestershire sauce, one tablespoon prepared mustard, one chopped green pepper, one-fourth teaspoon minced garlic, salt and pepper, dashes of nutmeg and cinnamon, and a half teaspoon of soda. This should be simmered for about an hour and should be stirred often.

When the salmon are running in the Umpqua, so many delicious salmon dishes appear at Grange pot lucks and food sales that an entire cook book could be written on salmon alone. One of my favorites is salmon croquettes, the creation of Dorothy Palmer, that superlative cook, that superlative neighbor. It is designed for the spring salmon which cannily appear in the river just at the time the first tender green peas reach perfection: To each pound of cooked salmon add two cups of hot mashed potatoes, a teaspoon and a half of salt and a proper amount of pepper, two well beaten eggs, two cups rolled dry bread crumbs and a grated onion if you like grated onion. Remove all the bones from the fish, add potatoes and the rest and form into balls. Fry in deep fat and serve with new peas.

Geographically, Scottsburg is as far off Broadway as you can get and still stay out of the Pacific Ocean, and theatrically speaking, it is even farther away. Yet, some of my most exhilarating moments in the theater have been experienced in front of the rickety stage and the curtain made of quilts strung on wires in the Grange Hall. When I first saw the sketches and plays, I confess I suffered dreadfully for the players and huddled down in my seat in a storm of self-consciousness and embarrassment. Everything about the productions, from make-up to costumes (Roy Lewis, emoting as Romeo, clad in long underwear with short, puffed-out pantaloons made of old drapes, must have set Shakespeare spinning in his grave), interpretation, and stage sets was indelibly home-made. I'm not embarrassed any more. The actors have a whale of a time and so does the audience.

No evening—not even the time the nice old lady representing "Whistler's Mother" in the living pictures sneezed and sent her false teeth flying across the stage—will ever compare with the night the "kiddies," God bless them, entertained us with a "Story Book Festival." The Three Bears were there, Wynken, Blynken and Nod, Goldilocks, the Tin Woodman and all the toys—Teddy bears, rag dolls, two Jack-in-the-boxes. The story line was fresh: a little girl goes to sleep and dreams the Good Fairy flies in the window and brings the toys to life, allowing them to sing and dance and recite, like the rare little hams they are.

Music was punched from the dilapidated piano and supplemented by an old fiddler and a young prodigy who squeezed an accordion. No sooner had the quilts parted and the music soared in ragged discord, than a dramatic squalling arose from one of the Jack-in-the-boxes. The six-year-old kid inside was suffering from claustrophobia,

108

which, when you stop to think about it, is about the worst phobia a Jack-in-the-box can have. The lid flew open and he popped out, dressed in a white clown's suit, with a ruffled collar and a pointed hat with a white pompom on top. "Lemme out!" he bawled. His tears were shatteringly real and his mother hurried toward the stage. The stricken actor tipped over his prison and crawled out. His white clown's uniform was stained a violent green from the crepe-paper lining of the box. "They made me be a Jack-in-the-box and I wet my pants and now I'm all green," the child wailed as his mother escorted him, none too gently, up the center aisle and out into the night.

The quilts flew together, the musicians regrouped and the whole thing started again. The curtains parted, the star said her piece, hit the sack, and started to dream on schedule. The Good Fairy glided in through the window, hung on a wire, waving her thin arms which were covered with gauze and tinsel wings. That is, the script called for her to glide in, but the stage hands zinged her across the stage and her golden wand caught in the quilt curtains. Then they tried to pull her back and stretched her out almost horizontally, about four feet above the stage. The strain was too much. The wire suspending the Good Fairy and the wires holding up the curtains broke in the same awful instant. The Good Fairy crashed in hysterics, leaped instantly to her feet, and, for no good reason, planted a round-house slap on the boy who manipulated the curtain. Goldilocks, his sister, grabbed a handful of Good Fairy hair and yanked. The Tin Woodman, caught up in the frenzy, smacked a Teddy bear with the flat of his wooden ax and Raggedy Ann sunk her fist in the middle of Wynken's Doctor Denton's. The Mad Hatter wrestled on the floor with two of the Three Bears and Little Miss Muffet roared off her tuffet and bit Little Jack Horner on the left arm. The place rocked with unrestrained whoops of the audience and the cries of parents whose children were engaged in public mayhem. Jimmy Van Natta dashed for the stage and hollered for the house lights. "I think that ends our performance tonight," he said sadly. "All the little toys have worked very hard and are awfully tired tonight." Behind Jimmy, we could see the little toys crying and belting each other in a general free-for-all. They didn't look tired to me.

If the Grange had no other reason for existing in the Umpqua—and there are thousands of good ones—its Christmas parties would justify it forever. The Christmas parties unify the valley, tying it together in the softest bonds of Christian charity and love. Then the hills and canyons empty, and lonely people, who may not see one another for months at a time, gather around the old grandfather stove (amidst the mob hysteria of the children) to talk of old times and new wonders. The talk at Christmas parties is the gentle, rambling conversation of old friends gathered in warmth to smile and watch the children and think of children of other years.

The party actually starts right after Thanksgiving Day when the Grange committees go to work. Loggers on the tree committee keep their eyes open as they range the forest for the perfect tree; lights burn brightly at Grange Hall night after night as the popcorn ball committee and the taffy committee go about their sticky work; Claude Sherman always comes down from Cottage Grove to supervise the laying of acres of peanut brittle; children string cranberries for the tree and the littlest ones fabricate chains of red and gold and green paper. Tin cans are cut and flattened and snipped into bright stars and curlicued trees and bangles; a committee goes to eastern Oregon where the big, foot-long pine cones grow. On the night when a long logging truck pulls up in front of Grange Hall with the tree, most of the valley turns out to help the committee. The tree is about eighteen feet tall and the men grunt and swear softly as they zigzag it through the front door and make it stand solidly in the corner. Evergreen branches and garlands of pine cones are strung on the walls.

The Grange Hall is very much Christmas Past, but the riotous, child-dominated present always wins. The stove glows warmly, the big room smells of popcorn and molasses, smells of slightly acid cranberries, of warm cider and evergreen boughs, of pastries and happy people. Santa Claus arrives in a jangle of bells and whoops of the children—the shy children down from the hills and the bold, "metropolitan" children of Scottsburg, some of whom have been as far away as Coos Bay. Santa's bag is filled with presents for every child. There are bean bags with faces embroidered on them; aprons for the little girls and rag dolls and monkeys made from gray socks with red toes; mittens and home-made jigsaw puzzles; popcorn balls and peanut brittle. There are great platters of sparkling red and green and silver cookies sitting around everywhere, cookies shaped like Santa Claus and horses and reindeer and gingerbread men, and anybody can have as many cookies as he wants any time he pleases.

Then, as the sated children begin to yawn, someone starts the music softly on the piano. A fiddle adds its whine, an accordion and a couple of harmonicas join the melody, and we sing. We sing carols and hymns of praise and wonder: "Silent Night, Holy Night," "Deck the Halls with Boughs of Holly," "Hark, the Herald Angels Sing," "Jingle Bells" and "White Christmas." The hall swells with our voices, swells to bursting with our fullness. The Grange Christmas party is the best party in the world.

One person, in particular, I was looking forward to meeting at the Grange. This was Mary Levenhagen who was the only woman in the valley with a special dispensation to be sick. She was in her usual place next to Sadie Andrews, and her husband, Paul, carried food in prodigious amounts to her. Mary was very fat, sallow of complexion and disposition, a dedicated and accomplished eater. It was well known that Mary was delicate. Mary Levenhagen as near as I could tell, had never done anything in her life except be delicate.

Mary and Paul Levenhagen were second-generation old timers and owned a large ranch on which they lived, in a decaying mansion in splendid sloth. Paul Levenhagen did all the housework and cooked and carried for Mary. Apparently, that was all that was done. The front porch and several rooms of their grand house had rotted away. They let it rot, nailed up the front door and used a back door for the rest of their days. When one room became unusable, they moved into the still-sound ones. The Levenhagen sheep ran unattended through the Levenhagen forest; coyotes took their share but Paul and Mary did not care: there were plenty of sheep. In the proper season, they hired men to round up the ewes and care for the new lambs, but not a Levenhagen muscle moved except in gentle to-and-fro patterns around the dining table and kitchen range.

There was one exception to the air of debility which filled this lethargic paradise. Whatever passion dwelt in Mary's soul was directed toward blue jays. Mary Levenhagen hated blue jays with a cold and unremitting fury. It is not recorded how Paul Levenhagen stood on jays but he had no choice. Every morning, under orders from Mary, he'd shoulder his gun and blast away at the jays. For some reason, the sight of a feathery blue corpse plumping to earth warmed Mary and filled her day.

When Paul Levenhagen died, there was wonder in the valley. What would poor Mary do? Poor Mary who had been an invalid all her life? Gard Sagaberd, her brother, could help some: but Mary remained the worry of the valley. But not for long. What Mary did, fooling us all, was to come to life. You could not say Mary was transformed into a blue streak, but she moved, she was mobile. She cooked her own leviathan meals and managed her life quite handily. The first thing she did was to get out in the yard and shoot blue jays. "Got twenty-two today," she told a neighbor who had come to commiserate with the stricken widow. "They sort of got ahead of me while Paul was sick." The second thing she did was to buy an automobile and whiz around the west—Crater Lake, California, eastern Oregon—and forget all about being an invalid. This lasted ten years. Then she joined Paul in the little cemetery on our hill.

Spring was with us for our induction into the Grange.

Inside the hall, masses of rhododendron and azalea covered the towering cylindrical stove; wild lilac and dogwood boughs were garlanded over the upright piano Emma Hedden's forebears had shipped around the Horn (the piano so frighteningly out of tune). I remembered my first cold, cold visit to the Grange and bundled up my soul, feeling, nevertheless, that things would be different this time. Pappy and I and Young Norman knew most of the people. The women no longer gave me the long eye, as they had on my previous sortie.

Jane Murphy, current master of the Grange, rapped for order. There was a special announcement to be made, she said.

Up stepped Maude Applegate and Ken Murphy, a committee of two appointed to procure coffee cups for the Grange. "We didn't have much money, as you know," Maude began, "so we shopped as carefully as we could. We went to Drain and we went to Reedsport and Coos Bay. Finally we saw an ad for a fire sale up at Eugene and Ken and I drove up there. Well, we arrived in a pouring rain and there must have been twelve million people milling around that place. Ken and I elbowed our way in and finally got hold of a clerk and he showed us the cups and saucers. They were fine—not hurt by the fire at all—and they cost about four dollars less than we had. We feel we got a real bargain and hope you will be pleased."

Ken Murphy bent his long frame and ripped the top off a large carton, revealing a mass of tissue paper. "They're sure packed nice," he said, plunging his hand in the rustling paper and feeling around for a cup. "Oh, my," he said, raising his face which had an odd, stricken look.

"Oh, my!" Maude Applegate reached into the carton and began to giggle. Then she pulled out a white brassiere and shrieked as she pointed to the printing on the carton, which none of us had noticed before. "B-CUPS," it said. The place exploded with laughter; Grangers slapped one another on the shoulder, they whooped and hollered and shouted. Ken Murphy, that gentle and modest man, blushed to the roots of his white hair. "I guess I picked up the wrong carton," he said, trying to explain against the tide of laughter. "It was on the loading dock and the clerk just told us to pick it up. It said 'Cups' on it and it was raining like billy hell so I just picked 'er up and drove away." Maude was convulsed: "I *thought* the carton seemed awfully light but when I said so Ken just said it wasn't nothing for an old Kentuckian like him." It was ten minutes before the sputtering crowd would calm down. Ken Murphy, still stricken by the enormity of his mistake, finally gave up trying to explain and just gazed in anguish at Jane, hoping for some sympathy. But his wife was laughing too hard to help him.

Something—a great deal, in fact—of the meaning of the Grange reached us on our induction night. "As members of this community," Jane told us with sincerity and simplicity, "you have both privileges and responsibilities. It is all summed up in one word and that word is 'neighborliness'. In a little, isolated community like Scottsburg, neighborliness is an absolute necessity. We don't have a police department. We don't have a fire department or an ambulance or a doctor within quick reach. We all are dependent on one another in case of emergency. Only by helping one another can we exist as a community."

115

Jane Murphy's open, pleasant face clouded as she thought how to drive the message deep. "There is no other way to live here except as neighbors," she continued. "If you are not a neighbor, you can never be a true member of this community or of this Grange." Then she smiled. "When you are called on for neighborly services, give freely and make your neighbor feel it is a joy for you to help. Then it *will* be a joy, a real joy."

Jimmy Van Natta, the self-confident, bright-eyed, gay fellow who had entered the valley several years before, was our sponsor. He was a landscape architect near Los Angeles before the valley claimed him. He loved the valley; now he spoke of things close to his heart, and he addressed the old-timers. "I want to talk to you folks who hold some of the original land grants because your ancestors came here first," Jimmy Van Natta began. "You own the land and the streams and the trees and whatever lies beneath the surface. All this is clear and legal. But in another sense you cannot own the land. It is yours only for a little time. Who can own a rainbow over a waterfall? Who owns the serenity we all feel watching night creep over these mountains or when the valley is filled with pink clouds at sunset? Who can buy or sell the grace of a deer or the strength of a salmon fighting up the river? We can't own these things because they belong to God. We can enjoy them for our short time on earth. Or we can destroy them. We can log off the hills. We can set fire to the woods. We can despoil the streams. We can leech out the goodness of the land, putting our fields to the wrong crops. If you kill the land, you will leave nothing but desolation after you."

There was an unaccustomed stillness in the room as his listeners realized that Jimmy Van Natta was finding words for something they had all felt. "It is a sin to log a hill and leave it barren," he continued, "covered with slash—ugly and subject to erosion. It is a sin to kill land by cropping out its goodness. And there is a third kind of sin: the sin of indifference as to what will happen to the land after it leaves your hands. When you sell land, as some of you are doing, I think you must make sure it will be bought by someone who will give it proper care. We can keep this valley a place of beauty and comfort and plenty —or we can destroy it."

Then he turned to us. "All these things involve you, too," he said, "because you have decided to be a part of the valley. I am glad to sponsor your membership, Gladys and Norman Workman and Norman Jackson, because you three have made your place in the community. It is good to welcome you as friends and neighbors."

Jimmy Van Natta would have laughed if anyone had called him a poet, but his quiet speech that night has always remained in my mind as poetry. (Gay, wise-cracking Jimmy was killed a few years later when a load of logs rolled off a truck and crushed him under the desperate weight.) There are other poets in the valley, mute poets, perhaps, men who have lived very intimately with the sky and the earth and the waters, who know every tree in their part of the forest and the ways of salmon and bobcat and elk.

I remember the time Harry Burchard decided to sell his land and retire. "I'm going to the city and take it easy," Harry said. A buyer was quickly interested in the lovely

Burchard land and a bargain had almost been reached when Harry stepped out onto his front porch to think through the final details. In a few minutes he returned. "I just thought of something I should have remembered," he said. "I can't sell this land."

The would-be buyer was aghast. "You mean you brought me all the way up here from Los Angeles and now you're backing out?"

"That's right," said Harry.

Later he confessed. "If I'd just stayed inside, everything would have been all right. But when I got outside and saw what a wonderful day it was, with the clouds rolling back and the sun sort of laying on the hills and the fox glove blooming all over the place, I just couldn't let go of it. That fellow was awful mad about it, but I did the right thing."

Paul Applegate is a man who understands how Harry Burchard feels. Paul is now in his seventies and has lived all but a few years within sight of the Umpqua. He is a very great hunter and woodsman, but lately he moves at a little slower pace. For one thing, he lost an eye while steelhead fishing a few years ago. "It was my aiming eye," he says, "and for a while I couldn't hit my hat." Not long ago, Pappy and Paul were going to drive to the town of Eugene, a trip Paul had been looking forward to for a long time. Pappy found Paul on his back porch, looking down at the river, just where the rapids start.

"You know, Norman," Paul said. "I sure wanted to go to Eugene up to a few minutes ago. But this is the first time in a week the sun's been out and I think I'll just sit here and watch the light change on the water and the way it hits those willows over there. I've seen a lot of days of clouds and sunshine here but this is one of the best. I'm going to sit here and enjoy it."

Pappy looked out to the river where a sudden fright of jumping chub minnows transformed the quiet surface into a sparkling of rings. He watched a loon slowly fly down the stream. "Move over," he said.

7

Bring Back
the Party Line

YOU CAN HAVE the modern telephone and welcome to
it. It leaves me cold. I know it is possible, in this miracle age of atoms and plastics, to sit in California and dial
New York. And get a wrong number. Or, if no one is home,
what you get is a noise which indicates a bell is ringing. It
isn't even a bell ringing; it's a transistored trick rigged to
sound like a bell ringing. The crazy part of all this is that
the people at the telephone company go around bragging
about their electronic gadgets. What they are hoping, ob-
viously, is that their bragging will make us forget how they
shamefully murdered the party line, unquestionably the
finest tool ever perfected for human communication. I'll
admit "perfected" may be a little strong. Actually, the
party line idea was never completely worked out, let alone
perfected, before it was throttled by an inferior thing
called Progress.

Nowadays, for instance, you must be home to receive a

telephone call. Preposterous! When we had a party line in the valley, every ring was heard at every instrument and you could pick up your calls anywhere you happened to be. Once, when I was in Emma Hedden's store in Scottsburg, I heard our call, four short rings. I went to the big box on the wall and answered. Mama was calling from Los Angeles. Pappy, who was nine miles away at Sawyer's Rapids, heard our ring and *he* answered, too. Young Norman was at Grandma Aurilla Butler's and, naturally, he came on the line. So we all had a chance to gabble with Mama. And not one of us was at home—where you have to be in these decadent, inefficient times, to make the phone work.

Even more marvelous (and deeply satisfying—at times) was the way the party line jumped in to solve everyone's problems. The day Mama broke her hip, I called Dr. Emboden in Drain, thirty-five miles east. Over the party line, of course. It seemed to me there were neighbors in the front yard wanting to help even before I had put the receiver back on the wall. The doctor arrived and gave Mama a pain-killing shot and we put her on a mattress in the station wagon and started to the hospital in North Bend, forty-five miles west. When we arrived at Reedsport, Don Yantis, the druggist, was in the street with a hypodermic the doctor needed. A state policeman was waiting, too, to escort us the rest of the way. We dreaded the long wait we would have at a spot in the road where they were removing a big chunk of mountain to widen the highway; we knew traffic was allowed to pass only a few minutes each day. But when we arrived the "road" had been cleared and we passed right through. At the hospital, two doctors were waiting and the X-ray room was ready.

The entire way had been smoothed by the good neighbors of the party line: once they knew Mama was seriously hurt, they summoned the state police, alerted the druggist, asked the highway workers to clear the road and notified the hospital. All I did was call the doctor; the party line did the rest! A few days later, Mama received a huge bouquet with a note. "The coffee sure is punk at the Workman ranch now that you're away," it said. "Please hurry home." It was signed, "Those guys on the county" —the big-hearted construction stiffs who had untied the road for her.

The quick flick of the helping hand was a characteristic of our party line. There was the rainy day Old Abe went bicycling into Scottsburg and entered Emma Hedden's store, looking as desolate as the weather. "Beautiful day; beautiful day," he said out of long habit. He exuded, beside his customary aroma, the smell of burned, wet wood.

"What've you been burning?" Emma asked. Old Abe seemed about to cry.

"Wup," he said, "my cabin burned down this morning. Whole thing. Everything burned up." He paused. "Wup, wup, saved the goats and the chickens. Stove fell. Burned everything. Wup, wup, wup, the worst part is I ain't got the money anymore. I had it in tin cans. Had cans full of money. Now I can't find where I put it."

"Of course, you've got money, you damned old idiot," Emma said. "Don't you remember we emptied all those cans and started you a bank account? Anyway, I don't think you're going to need money."

Emma came out of the post office section of the store and lifted the receiver on the box telephone near the door. "Who's on?" she asked. Several voices chirped up. All Emma said was, "Old Abe's cabin burned last night. Let's do something about it." For the next hour, the bell rang constantly. Listening to the signals (two shorts and three longs, Maude Applegate; three longs and a short, Maggie Burton; four longs . . .) Emma knew the word was spreading. Then the calls started coming back to Emma:

"Billy Hansen has a chicken house he doesn't use any more."

"We're going to put a couple of windows in the chicken house."

"Some of the fellows are making skids so we can move it."

"I've got some curtains and I asked the fellows to cut the windows to fit."

Before nightfall, the party liners had borrowed a tractor from a logger and dragged the chicken house to Old Abe's canyon (luckily the river was low enough so they could use the sturdy summer bridge) and set it solidly on a foundation of field stone. They whitewashed the walls, put up curtains, and installed a bed, a rocking chair and a small wood stove. They laid in a supply of flour, bread, preserves, cookies, some bacon and potatoes and canned goods. They supplied towels, wash cloths and napkins. "Wup, wup, wup, looks like I got me a hope chest," snickered Old Abe. "Regular hope chest." A few days later he wheeled into our yard. "Beautiful day," he said. "Wup, you ought to see my new place. Bet the king of England ain't got no finer. Ain't letting the goats in that house now. Gahdam dirty goats."

I scarcely know how to put this delicate matter, but it has to be faced: some people listened to party line calls which were, strictly speaking, none of their business. For as long as the party line lasted, arguments raged over this popular pastime. One school of thought said flatly that listening in on another's conversation was illegal—probably a Federal offense—but no one ever wanted to find out what the lawbooks said, if anything. A small group argued that eavesdropping simply was not "decent." They were for decency. Others contended it was only the neighborly thing to do. Still others, practical souls, said they didn't care whether anyone listened in or not—except that every receiver lifted from an unauthorized hook sucked a bit more power off the line and when too many nosey damn fools were listening, nobody could hear. That was certainly true. When the party line had a full house, you sometimes could not hear the party you called. But there was a practical solution for that. The ones who *could* hear always were glad to relay the conversation back and forth across the line and the messages always squeezed through. I whole-heartedly joined the Big Ear, or neighborly school, on two grounds: they were going to listen anyway, and they improved the service by serving as relay stations.

Mary Levenhagen was the valley's champion eavesdropper. She had her receiver on a long extension cord with a shoulder rest to hold it to her ear while she sat at ease in her padded rocker. Mary also had a cut-off device which silenced the noises of her house. Mary's silencer was a thoughtful thing. Usually, people who listened in poured the household noises surrounding them onto the line. One eavesdropper had a clock with a very loud tick and the bang, bang, bang of the clock always announced her presence in your conversations. Another listener rocked and rocked and *rocked* in a chair with a piercing, irritating squeak. Others could be picked out by the cadence of their breathing or an occasional cough. Our conversations were always very popular because we received so many long distance calls. One night, I was called from Chicago. It was impossible to hear because the volunteers were pulling all the power from the line. All I could get clearly was the sound of the squeaking chair, the tick-tock of the loud-mouth clock, and a new entry, a fellow with a very bad case of sniffles. Chicago and I finally managed a barely-audible connection but every time the sniffly one sniffled we were drowned out completely. At last I said, "For goodness sake, blow your nose. We'll wait, so you won't miss anything." "Okay, Gladys," he said. We waited a few minutes and when he returned, he said, "All set here," and Chicago and I went on with the world's business.

Mary Levenhagen was the only one on the line who made no bones about listening; she was always on the line; it was a way of life for her. If you wanted Mary, all you did was to pick up the receiver and say, "Mary, I haven't been able to get Muriel Monson all day. Do you know where she is?" Mary, not at all abashed, would usually know. "She and Andy went up to Drain this morning," she'd say. "They'll be back right after dinner." Mary was the chief target of the anti-eavesdroppers, the pleaders for "decency." But when she died, the valley suddenly realized it had lost a permanent, built-in ear which served everyone. "I don't know what I'm going to do," said Genevieve Smith. "All I had to do was talk to Mary and I knew everything happening in the valley."

The party line fascinated outsiders. A Seattle flower broker once called Norman; I answered. "Holy Smoke," he said, "that valley is sure jumping today, isn't it?"

"What do you mean?" I asked.

"You mean you haven't heard? Well, there's been an auto wreck down by the bridge in Scottsburg, and some woman is going on about having a baby, and somebody else called the doctor at Drain for her, and the fire warden came on the line and said he'd drive her to the doctor. A couple of other guys said they'd take care of the men hurt in the accident. A woman is raising hell with her man because he's forgotten what he was supposed to bring from the store in Reedsport, and Paul Wessela caught two steelhead."

"How in the world do you know all this?"

"Well, I called just about the time the accident happened and I guess the operator forgot all about me. I just hung on and listened."

"At long distance rates?"

"Sure, why not? That's a lively little burg you got going down there." Then he got to business, inquiring about a price he and Pappy had agreed to a week or so before. "Oh, golly," I said. "I don't pay too much attention, but I think it was ten dollars."

"Oh, no, Gladys," said a new, unidentified woman's

voice. "You've got it wrong. The price was ten dollars and a half that day. I'm real interested in things like that and I keep a list of prices every day. That was a pretty bad wreck. A couple of fellows from Elkton hit the steel part of the bridge and they're pretty bad off."

The wonder of the party line was that it existed at all. It looped and wandered in great scallops over twenty-five miles of the valley, attached here to a pole, there to a tree, here dragging along atop of willow and blackberry fields. In its halest moments, it had a self-conscious, apologetic voice. In crisis, which was often, its voice was a sickly thread—like the pulse of a dying man. It was beset by many ills and injuries. Bears tore the wire down; sometimes the poles sprouted in a valiant effort to regain their status as trees; woodpeckers attacked the poles; squirrels chewed insulation; sometimes bear or elk, scratching themselves against the poles, would send the line singing through the forest; loggers swiped wire to hold their equipment together—just as earlier loggers had cut wire to repair their harnesses. When it rained, the party line faltered, stumbled and often (alas!) fell prostrate. When it snowed, the unhappy line sagged under the weight of ice and snow and usually, reluctantly, inevitably broke. One lady, no longer young, blames the phone for blighted love. "One snowy night, a handsome logger I had been seeing was talking real sweet to me and I knew he was just about to ask me to marry him—since he couldn't get through the snow and all—when something broke and the line went dead," she says, happy to perpetuate the legend. "I'd have had him, too, with all them witnesses listening.

I guess he got scared because I never did hear anything sweet from him again after the line got fixed."

The reedy voice of the party line was the responsibility of Agnes Hudson, owner and operator (with her two handsome, tall daughters, Evelyn and Oretha) of the Elkton Telephone Co. Agnes Hudson, one of the most respected and loved women of the valley, is tall, too, and slender, has beautiful nut-brown skin from being out of doors so much, and a lovely complexion which sets off her steel-gray hair. She is a devout woman and only rarely uses language employed by linesmen. Whenever the line broke down, however, it was Agnes who supervised repairs, riding backward on a mule and paying out copper wire as the animal advanced up hill and down vale. She and Evvie and Retha were expert pole climbers and knew most of the tricks of the linesman's trade.

Agnes and her daughters were devoted to the party line and gave extraordinary service: Agnes Hudson could be depended on for recipes and expert advice on the construction of a baby's formula; she knew the comings and goings of the community and frequently refereed neighborhood arguments. She made a point of keeping track of the course of valley pregnancies, and when the time drew near cheerfully kept the line, which normally closed at eight in the evening, open for night calls. Agnes Hudson's super-service was also available for non-subscribers. One night, an agitated man ran to her home to announce his wife, who lived far away in the hills, was hemorrhaging and needed a doctor quickly. "Get back up there," Agnes said. "I'll get a doctor." She called Dr. Ber-

tha De Vore in Drain. "I don't know where she lives," said
Dr. Bertha. "We'll find it," said Agnes and waited down
the road in a downpour to meet Dr. Bertha. It had been
raining for several days and there were slides on the highway, but the two women tackled the almost non-existent
road into the twisting canyon. When they returned it was
dawn, but the patient had been saved.

As though she did not have enough to do, Agnes once
insisted that an elderly couple, also dwelling far back in
the hills, should have a telephone. "Granny" had often
told Agnes how worried she was. "My man's awful sick,"
she said. "I sure don't want him to die up there on the hill.
Course, my boy lives only a little ways up the road,
but. . . ."

"You've got to have a phone," Agnes interrupted.
"Retha and Evvie and I want to put one in. We won't
charge you." Agnes was puzzled because every time she
mentioned the phone installation, Granny looked con-
fused and worried; she simply "froze" and would talk no
more. So Agnes Hudson took the matter into her own
hands and appeared at Granny's cabin with the necessary
tools to install a phone.

She looked around the cabin which had two bedrooms
and a general kitchen-dining-sitting room. "Where do
you want the phone?" she asked. Granny was silent and
then, unexpectedly, began to cry softly. "I want it outside
the house somewheres," she sobbed. By gentle prying,
Agnes learned what was troubling the old lady. The
couple's son, who lived not far away, had rigged an inter-
communication system between the two houses. He had
put the speaker in the bedroom where the old gentleman

slept. But instead of running the connecting wire around the corners of the room, or along the floor, he had strung it through the window and directly across the room to the speaker.

"The thing is," said Granny, wiping her teary eyes, "Paw has his trouble with his kidneys and he has to get up two or three times every night. And every time Paw gets up"—she started to sob again—"he forgets, and that wire clips him under the chin and flips him over. That's why I don't want another wire running around in here. If my old man takes many more falls, it'll kill him, and it drives me to distraction every time he hits the floor."

Such forays into the hills were over and above the call of duty, but the ordinary, day-in-day-out performance of Agnes Hudson's line was astonishing. I was in Chicago when a friend announced he was heading for Oregon and wanted to know how the fishing was. "I'm just going to call home," I said. "I'll find out for you." I picked up the hotel phone. "I'm going to call Scottsburg again," I announced to the operator. "Oh, fine, Mrs. Workman," she said. "You just go right ahead." (The hotel operators had tangled with the party line a couple of times and had learned to leave it to me.)

After a few minutes, Agnes Hudson came on the line. My long distance operator asked for our number and said it was a collect call. "Oh, that must be Gladys," said Agnes. "Tell her Pappy's not at home. He's gone down to the Palmers."

"Ask her to transfer the call to the Palmers, please," I asked.

"Oh, I forgot," said Agnes. "They're not there, either.

They ate early and went up to Eugene to the fights." No chance of getting Norman, but Mom Kruse in Yoncalla would know about the fishing. I asked for her number. Agnes came on again. "They're not home, either," she said. "The whole lot of them went up to Eugene to the basketball game."

I thought for a moment. "Well, I've got to get someone to tell me about the fishing. Please transfer me to Gus Peret."

"There's no use calling Gus," Agnes reported. "He hasn't been fishing. Anyway, the fishing isn't any good. The stripers aren't hitting, it's too late for trout and the salmon haven't started running yet."

"Thanks and cancel the call," I said, mentally reviewing my bag of information. Item: Norman had a good dinner at the Palmers; much, much better than he could have cooked for himself. Item: Barney Smith, a valley welterweight, was boxing at Eugene; otherwise Pappy would not have gone to the fights. Item: Reta, Mom Kruse's great-granddaughter, and the Yoncalla High basketball team were playing at Eugene. Otherwise, the Kruse tribe would not have gone. Item: Gus Peret, the photographer, must have company. Otherwise, he certainly would have been fishing. I turned to my friend.

"The fishing is terrible," I said.

The valley party line had been performing such brilliant services since 1898 when the first, stuttering, battery-powered line was strung from Elkton to below Scottsburg. Rock Freyer, who had worked putting the line up, remembered: "We didn't bother with poles so much then,"

he said. "We just warped her to the trees." The line was
the proper wonder of the valley. No longer was it necessary to hitch up the horses and take to the canyons to
communicate. The men and women of the valley were
immediately—if precariously—linked; furthermore, they
had a window to the outside world: now there was a way
in and a way out of the valley beside the ponderous old
stern-wheeler or the jolting pitch by wagon on the old
plank road over the mountain to the east. The unexpected
and delightful thing, however, was that the party line
furnished entertainment, too. Old Uncle Billy, the best
fiddler in the valley, would scrape away at popular tunes
while all the valley listened. Later, when a phonograph
was imported, the party liners heard the excruciatingly
funny Uncle Josh records, and "The Night the Dog Died"
and, when they came along, "The Two Black Crows."

Of course, the party line suffered from lack of pep, ane-
mia and general fag then even worse than in its later years,
and it was always a frustrating problem for a subscriber
at one end to burrow through the intermediate ears to
reach the designated listener. And, almost from the first,
the principal relay station was manned by Aurilla Butler,
now in her eighties, and called Grandma Butler or Aunt
Ralia by everyone in the valley. Aurilla married Abraham
Butler (Ham Butler, everyone called him) something over
sixty years ago and moved into the house where she still
lives, a house about midway on the party line. Grandma
Butler is round and plump and wears her soft hair in a bun
which sits precisely on top of her head. ("A woman's hair
is her crowning glory, and why they ever want to whack it
off is more than I can see.") Her face is covered with the

tiniest, finest wrinkles and she has a soft, quiet voice everyone recognizes. Grandma Butler goes to everything that happens in the valley and she is the inventor and perfector of the apple custard pie which will insure her immortality. The party line was a big part of Grandma Butler's life. On days when the line's voice faded and squeaked, two short rings would fetch Grandma to the phone. Then, serving as a sort of conversational midwife, she would extract the conversation and fit it together to establish communication. On very bad days, Grandma would give up her regular duties to stick close to the phone where she knew she would be needed. She was more efficient and ten times pleasanter than any additional power source on the line could ever be.

In shared joys and sorrows, in all our moods, the party line tied us together. None of us will ever forget the black day when the line carried the ominous warning against a tragedy which could not be avoided. Pappy and I were standing outside talking to the driver of a logging truck when we heard the phone ringing sharply and incessantly. "Something's wrong," said the driver. "You can always tell when it sounds like that." We ran inside and picked up the phone. At first there was a mixed babble of voices:— "He looks like he's drunker than a lord."—"Can't anybody stop him?"—"Where is he now?" And then the chilling fact: "There's a guy coming up from Reedsport driving one of those great big gasoline tanker rigs all over the road. Unless he kills himself first, he's going to kill someone else just as sure as you're born. Get the children away from the highway and stay away yourself." The log truck driver with us hastily ran his truck into our field. Traffic through the valley, never heavy, slowed to a halt. The party line shouted bulletins: "He just barely got through Scottsburg," someone reported. "One of the double wheels got in that ditch in front of Emma's house. He was clear over on the wrong side of the road and it's a wonder he didn't turn over there and burn up the whole town." The tanker roared past the Lewis's, past Paul Applegate's place and avalanched through Green Acres, the new trailer and gas station settlement. Now we could hear the approaching rumble. There was nothing to do and nothing to say. We just watched silently as the wavering tanker thundered past our house and disappeared. We listened for a while, listened for the crash we all expected as the tanker slammed up the highway toward Elkton and Drain. "He's just come by here going like a bat out of hell," Sawyer's Rapids reported. Then there was another period of waiting. Silence. Surely, we all thought, there has been time for him to clear the valley. When the phone rang, we jumped to our feet. It was Grandma Butler. "That tanker tangled with a car just before it got into Elkton," she said. "All I know is two people are dead."

When we talk about the year of the snow in the valley, people give us patronizing looks as though it never happened. It did, though. It had rained for weeks and the sides of the mountains, heavy with moisture, slid down into the river, blocking the road in a dozen places. Then the thermometer dropped and the rain stopped. In the bitterly cold nights, you could hear the fir trees cracking, like the sound of guns, as their boughs froze and snapped;

the sound of gigantic musketry filled the valley. In those hours, it seemed as though the elements were towering unseen above us, poised for another blow.

Then about ten days before Christmas, it began to snow. The first peculiar thing about the snow was that the storm was aimed directly at us. There was no snow at Elkton or Reedsport, the gates of the valley, but at Scottsburg it snowed day after day. The second peculiar thing was the snow was blue. If you ventured outside and struggled through the drifts, the hollows left by your feet were blue, almost indigo blue. None of us had ever seen such a thing and, in the first day, before the party line floundered and died, we all discussed it. (Ken Murphy said later he read somewhere blue snow was caused by thousands and millions of insects, somehow caught in the stuff, but none of us put much stock in that, not even Ken.) It was magnificently beautiful but the blueness, reflected everywhere we looked, lent an added sense of mystery to the unusual storm. The weight of the snow flattened a small house in Scottsburg and crushed one of Emma's storehouses. Living things gave up. There was almost no movement in the valley except for the wisps of smoke that drifted from our chimneys and added its blueness to the scene. The trees themselves, century-old firs, gave up. The crushing weight of the snow on their limbs pushed downward against the roots, which grappled with the sodden ground and could not hold. Trees as high as ten story buildings silently began to move, remaining almost perpendicular as they slid down the mountain slopes and then toppled with a volcanic crashing which was somehow muffled, yet magnified, by the snow. The valley became an eerie and unfamiliar place and we were tense and alert.

Then the snow stopped and silence really clamped down. For days there was no car on the road. Far, far away we heard snow plows droning. Suddenly, the party line jangled in the silence. We were in the land of the living again! Someone, which hardy soul I never learned, had plodded through chest-high drifts to put the line in order. It was then we all thought, for the first time: this year there would be no Christmas party at the Grange. No gathering of neighbors, no Christmas tree, no peanut brittle, no rag dolls and cookies. Only a few people could reach the hall and only a few people were not enough for the party.

On the night the party had been scheduled, however, people drifted into our house, the ones from a few miles around who could get to us. I've forgotten now just who was there. Maude and Paul Applegate and Christine Lewis were there, Pansy and Thode Andrews, Preacher Gus Nickander, Emma Hedden, Mae and Jimmy Van Natta and a few others. The house was warm and smelled like Christmas, and every package and pot the guests brought added to the aroma: pies and cakes and venison roasts, green rice and creamed chicken were lined up on the stove. The bouquet of hard candy and egg nog, fir wreaths and good coffee filled the air, and our pot-belly stove staved off the cold. We toasted the season and talked of the wonders of the weather and ate too much of every good dish and wondered about the other people in the valley. "Let's call up the people on the party line," suggested Mae Van Natta. "We can at least be with them for a few minutes." We took turns talking to everyone on the line and then Preacher Gus said quietly, "Tell everyone to stand by. We'll have some singing."

Big Preacher Gus Nickander, the valley carpenter, stood proud and tall before us, his shoulders broader than ever as he raised his hands and led us. He is a simple and proud man and he made us sing simply and proudly that night, singing with our neighbors of the party line. There was no accompanying music except the melody we carried in our hearts. We sang the old, old songs. We sang of shepherds on a far-away hill and the star and the little Babe of Bethlehem; we sang of kings out of the east and what happened in a manger on a bright and silent night. We sang of angels and halls of holly, of jingling sleigh bells and hope and human warmth and kindness and joy to the world. The room filled with our spirit and our hearts swelled for our neighbors. Long after the singing was over, our signal jingled from the phone and when we lifted the receiver, it was neighbors, telling us in commonplace, suddenly radiant, words of their joy shared with us and of their thanks.

I was pretty high on the party line after that performance and I'm afraid I gushed a little. I was telling Gard Sagaberd and old Rock Freyer about it all at the store a few days after Christmas when I remembered Rock had been one of the first men to use the party line. "Was it as wonderful then as it is now?" I burbled. "What was the first thing you ever heard over the party line?"

Rock jumbled his knobby face into thought. Then he smiled. "I remember now," he said. "It was 'Hello.'"

8

Please, Don't Call It Pottery

THAT GREAT SHOCK of fine brown hair Pappy wore when we were married has drifted away; his hair is now sparse and gray. But his compassionate eyes—back of spectacles now—still look at me a little quizzically. A friend once said, "If there isn't a heaven, they'll have to invent one for Norman Workman," and I believe it. I was just a little girl when we first met and I think Pappy still regards me pretty much as a little girl who should be allowed to do anything that pleases her. What makes him a candidate for a hand-tooled, monogrammed heaven is the fact he doesn't go around second-guessing when I fall on my face; most times, he seems to see or sense some grain of logic in my schemes. Pappy has survived and even enjoyed my alarms and excursions. When I inadvertently got myself in conjunction with ceramics, the explosion rocked Pappy: he bent, he wavered in the shock wave but, even then, he didn't break.

It all started as calmly as tea at the rectory. Stella Hardy called from Los Angeles where she had been confined many months caring for her ill parents. "I just got a reprieve," she said. "I'm going to get out of here for a couple of weeks."

"Wonderful," I cried. "Come up here."

"Do you want to take ceramics?" Stella asked.

"Pottery?" I mused. "Sure, I'll get some people together. You come up here and teach us all you want."

"Don't call it pottery," said Stella primly, "ceramics."

I called Maggie Burton first. "Maggie, how'd you like to take ceramics?"

"Gee, kid," Maggie said. "I don't see why I wouldn't. I've taken Serutan and Lydia Pinkham's and about everything else. What's ceramics good for?"

"It's great for the nerves," I said, "but you can't take it alone. I'm trying to get a class of ten together." Maggie and I got a class of ten lined up for Stella in no time at all; everyone seemed hipped on the idea of making pottery, even though it had to be called ceramics.

In due time, Stella Hardy arrived, bearing ceramic clay, fragile greenware—the thin, moulded and dried clay we were to color and glaze and fire and finally prize as works of art. I was not there to meet her; my heart had gone sour again and I was in the hospital when ceramics invaded the valley; I was sick all during Stella's artistic visitation and learned nothing at all of ceramics and its evident charms. The others, however, were enthusiastic about the new art and happily followed Stella through the steps which produced flowers and bowls and miniature

140

figures. Unfortunately, Stella was called back to Los Angeles by a crisis in her father's illness. She left the valley hurriedly, but her students were well pleased, I thought, not to say entranced, with their new accomplishments. And I must say I was entranced, too, when they showed me their work.

It was not until months later that I discovered some of Stella's pupils were muttering and unhappy about the course. The rumble caught up with me in Coos Bay, just before the daffodil-picking season. An acquaintance met me on the street. "They're saying some awful things about you, Gladys," she said. "Some of the bud pickers are saying they don't think they'll pick for you this year if you don't do better by them than you did by the people in the ceramics class."

"I don't see how they could be unhappy," I said. "They made everything they were supposed to before Stella left." But the grumbling continued. From Elkton to Coos Bay, from Reedsport to Coquille, wherever the four winds blow. It did not hit me directly again, however, until the church bazaar in Elkton. We were just leaving the big room where the weak winter sun struck through the amber windows and the smell of pastries and good coffee filled the air, when a lanky young woman with startlingly blue eyes and sandy hair placed herself solidly in front of me. She looked as big as a lady Paul Bunyan.

"You're the jane who had those fancy ceramics classes, ain't you?" she asked. "Where the girls never had a chance to finish?" The other ladies gathered round. It was very quiet. "Not only that," continued the giantess, "but all those girls bought a lot of supplies and what are they supposed to do with them now?" Without advance warning, I went all weak and started to cry.

"I don't know what I can do," I sobbed. "Would it be all right if I bought back the stuff they have?"

Another harpy spoke up. "Might have known you'd say something like that," she sniffed. "Trying to make the whole thing right with your money. Well, the longer you live in this valley you'll find money won't buy friendship. And you're going to find a lot of us won't be on hand to pick your buds."

Some kind soul stepped up and put her arms around me. "Don't worry, Gladys, it's not as bad as they say. Don't even listen to them."

I stopped crying and got mad. "No," I said, "let's get this out in the open. I'm sick of hearing about it. First of all, the ceramics class has nothing to do with daffodils. But you seem to think it does, so I'll tell you what I'm going to do. If you come and pick for us, I'll go to Los Angeles, right now, and take ceramics lessons from the best teachers I can find, and I'll come back and teach any of you who think you didn't get a fair deal—and I'll teach free."

"Huh!" said the lanky girl. That "huh" had more eloquence than the collected speeches of Winston Churchill. I flew home and told Pappy of my plan. All he said was, "I just don't think you are well enough to go." "I'm going," I said. And, right in the middle of the picking season, I went.

I plunged into a new and mysterious world—a world of engobe (AHNgobe), the first kind of underglaze paint we had, very thick and difficult to work with; slip, the clay used for casting; pugged clay, for modeling; potters wheels; glazes; over-glazes; kilns. I learned to cast slip in plaster moulds to make greenware; I learned how to fire the greenware until it emerged from the kiln as pure white bisque; I learned to make flowers almost as beautiful as those in the garden. All this, I learned under the tutelage of Gladys Burbank at the Willoughby studio in Los Angeles. I went to class every day and I followed Gladys Burbank when she went to San Diego to teach. Gladys Burbank, about five feet two, with dark brown hair and dark brown eyes, attacked ceramics with joy. She rarely spoke an unnecessary word but she had the born teacher's knack of showing just what we had to learn. I studied under her for three months and then sortied back to the Umpqua, ready to teach. And I toted back over nine hundred dollars' worth of ceramics supplies.

Shortly before I went to Los Angeles to learn to become a professor of ceramics, we had moved into a fishing shack about two miles up the road toward Elkton. It was a solid little house, standing—like a chorus girl on long skinny legs—above the river in a clump of firs. When I returned, Pappy and Norman and Claude Sherman had glassed in the big screened sleeping porch, and installed a big pot-belly stove in the combination living-dining room, an attic, which made an unfinished bedroom, and a lean-to bedroom downstairs. The chorus girl legs had been covered demurely with siding and the place had a fine, well-lived-in look.

In Los Angeles, whenever my heart had growled at me, I'd slapped it down with pills and tough talk but, for a spell after I returned to the valley, the pesky thing forced me into bed again. That did not stop forward progress. We simply moved my bed to the big porch, covered the spread with a plastic sheet, and started school. The first call went out to the disgruntled girls from Elkton who felt Stella (and I) still owed them something, but the gruntled came too. Salmon season was on and I became an object of curiosity to the fishermen on the river. They could see me propped up in bed on the porch doing some mysterious thing, and more and more of them dropped in to see what was going on.

It is my luck I had not taken time out to think about ceramics and me. In a moment of panic and anger, I had promised to learn ceramics and teach the few who thought Stella had gypped them. In my mind, I never went beyond that point. And when the time came when all agreed all debts had been paid in full, we were simply too busy to sit around cogitating about the future. Before that first class was over, we had been persuaded to start two more. We were surrounded by eager ladies, determined to commit something in clay. I graduated from the bed to a bridge table. Then Norman and Claude Sherman built a table twenty-six feet long on the porch. The men built drying racks around the pot-belly stove in the living-dining room. They built drying racks in the kitchen. Stacks of moulds and greenware littered the house. When the greenware reached the bathroom, Young Norman called a halt. "I'm not going to have a bunch of white madonnas in there watching me take a bath," he stormed, "we've got to have one room where we can get away from ceramics."

Normal people must have thought we were demented to live in such a state and I am amazed, myself, to think things went on this way for almost two years before we realized we had to have more space. We bought two houses from the war-time conscientious-objectors camp down the road. They soon overflowed with ceramics supplies. We built a two-car garage and filled that up. We finally built a studio building, about the size of a five-room house and moved the whole ceramics business out of our own house.

We had classes every day of the week—morning and night. And every day, it seemed, more people showed up for classes. We ordered a railroad carload of ceramic clay (and stored it in Portland and Eugene so our customers could be served quickly). The kilns—we had five of them —ran day and night. We were appointed distributors for ceramic supplies, for kilns and tools, glazes and moulds. Young Norman cast greenware until his arms ached. Pappy kept the books. I tried to keep one jump ahead of the students.

In those years, hobby ceramics was just beginning its zoom to national popularity. And, in those years, the experts guarded their secrets like a bunch of alchemists. It was traditional for anyone who had perfected a certain process to guard his treasure. I never had any secrets. For one thing, my students knew what my training was and I didn't try to fool them. Many times we would work together to perfect a new technique. "I can't figure out why we pay you good money," Mary Colley of Elkton laughed one day. "All you do is let us show *you* how things should be done." Any time I heard of something new, I'd beat my way to Los Angeles to try to find out how it was done. On one flying trip, I was introduced to a glorious pink glaze which could be combined with a brown to produce a wonderful rosy-bronze finish. Back in the valley, however, the pink glaze did us false: for months the valley was flooded with hideous, bilious pink objects fresh from our kiln.

Still the students came. They arrived in house dresses and in furs; they arrived in pickup trucks and Cadillacs. They came from a radius of 150 miles. They came in the morning and they came at night. The morning classes, with time out for lunch, were supposed to end at two in the afternoon, but we could never devise a way to make the students leave. Our morning classes ran into the evening classes which started at seven. Many, many times, the evening classes would not break up until one in the morning. Sometimes students stayed all night. They ranged from ladies from the backwoods of the Smith River country to a genuine refugee from Park Avenue. We had fat ones and slim ones, noisy ones and quiet ones, the blatantly sacrilegious and the devout.

The "Tuesday Class" was one of my favorites. It started when a thin, quietly—and expensively—dressed lady knocked on the front door. It took me a while to locate her since no one ever uses our front door, preferring to come barreling in the back way. I asked her in. "Maybe it would be better if we talked in the yard for a moment," she said. "You've got a lot of people in there now." We stepped out under the crabapple tree. "I hear you teach people to make pottery," she said.

I gestured toward the stacks of moulds and ceramic clay which lay in the yard. "Well, yes," I said.

"My name is Miss Violet and I run a place on the waterfront in a nearby coast town." She handed me a card: *Imported Specialties for Men.* "I might as well tell you, it isn't a haberdashery," said Miss Violet. "Lately, I've been getting a very high-type girl and there's nothing for them to do in off hours. I was wondering if they could come up here and have a class in ceramics. It would give the girls something to occupy their time."

"I don't see why not," I gulped. "As far as I know, ceramics is good for everybody."

"You're sure it won't make any difference here in the valley?" Miss Violet asked. "What will the other ladies think?"

"Who's going to tell them?" I asked. "Are you?"

"Not likely," said Miss Violet.

Although there was a rather heavy turnover in personnel, the girls from Miss Violet's came to class every Tuesday for more than two years. And they were exquisitely and unfailingly polite.

The oddest thing about the whole ceramics business, at first, was that many women paid their fees for lessons and attended classes regularly but never made a move toward learning ceramics. They just wanted to be around, part of the sociable groups which had taken over our home and our lives. Somewhere in that first year we adopted a slogan, "Ceramics for Fun," and that has always been our goal. Along with the fun, some students have turned out exceptionally brilliant work, rivaling the finest por-

147

celains of Europe and the Far East. Some of the best work was produced by an improbable group which always stopped at the beer parlor on their way to class and arrived in a mild glow and a cloud of loud talk. A cardinal rule of ceramics is that clay and grease do not mix; if grease or hand lotion gets on the clay, it makes a slick spot which will not take color or glaze. But these geniuses would sit at the long table, most of them wearing sweaters (not advisable because lint and overglaze also do not mix), reaching into paper bags for doughnuts and greasy hot dogs. Flicking lint, manipulating the clay with their greasy hands, laughing and seemingly paying little attention to what they were doing, these delightful zanies somehow produced faultless results.

Then came Ruthie. I had a new class from north of Drain and as I went out to the porch to get started, I noticed that one of the chairs was empty. A wonderfully pneumatic-looking blonde saw my glance and spoke up. "That's for Ruthie. She'll be here." Before I could turn to the class, Ruthie bounded through the back door. Three cats streamed in after her. "Halloween's early this year," I thought. Ruthie was small and dark and wore her black hair in a Dutch bob, the bangs draping down almost to her eyebrows. Her mouth turned down at the corners. She looked mean and she sounded mean but I've since learned it's just the look of her: there's not a mean bone in her body. She fixed the blonde with a dark and fiery eye.

"Ah gawd, kid," she said with great bitterness. "Ah'm goin' to kill thet man of mahn effen it's the last thang ah ever do."

"Oh, come on, Ruthie," said the blonde gal. "Sit down and let's get on with the lesson. Meet the teacher."

Ruthie flashed me a quick black look. "Ah an't ennarested in meetin' no teacher," she said. "Ah only come because ah said ah would an' ah'm goin' to tell you all somethang an' then ah'm goin' home an' kill mah man."

Ruthie certainly had her audience! The class sat as though they were frozen, eyes clamped to Ruthie's face. "Last nat," she continued, "ah fixed supper lak always an' thet man never did show up. Ah mean he didn't show up all nat. Come daylat, he come draggin' in all covered with mud. He looked lak he'd been fallin'-down-drunk. 'You been over to thet redhead floozie's place?' ah asked him. 'You been fallin' down in them puddles down by her place?'

"He jest looks at me for a minute. Then he says, 'Shet up, woman. Ah been helpin' the boss git a cat down off the mountain.' Well, hale, ah knowed thet was a lie 'cause ef ary man hates cats, it's mah man. Ah grabbed thet ol' twelve-gauge gun an' ah said to him. 'Ah know all bout you an' cats an' ah know what kind of mountain you been workin' on an' ah'm goin' over there an' pull ever' red hair off her floozie head. But, first, ah'm goin' to kill you.'"

"Ah, now, Ruthie," said the big blonde, "don't you know he was just talking about a caterpillar tractor? That's the only kind of cat he was talking about."

Ruthie turned her furious eyes on the blonde. "My frind," she said. "Ah will kandly thank you to shet up. Well, thet man jest looked at me for a spell. Then he said, 'We got a pretty good slide when thet cat was about half-way up the mountain an' the boss was afraid she'd slide

149

all the way an' bury thet cat. So he says he'd give twenty-fahve dollars to ennaone who'd get thet cat down. So ah git an idea thet we could jest hook a donkey onto thet cat an' drag her down thet way. Well, thet's jest what we done. We got a wahr on the cat an' hooked onto the donkey an' then thet damn donkey wouldn't go. So the boss offered enother fahve dollars to ennaone who'd keep the donkey goin' an' ah went up there an' did it.'

"Ah tol' him thet was one thang ah could understand. 'You goin' up to thet donkey is jest lak one jackass meetin' enother,' ah said. He come over lak he was goin' to hit me an' ah raised thet gun an' said, 'Keep talkin'.' 'Damn effen you an't the sorriest damn woman ah ever see,' he said. 'Ennaway, ah got thet donkey goin' an' the boss give me the thirty dollars an' he said he'd never seen nothin' lak how ah did it. An' ah said it wasn't nothin', 'cause the only thang ah did was go up there an' goose thet donkey. Cross my hort, thet's the truth.'

"Ah gawd, kid," continued Ruthie to her blonde friend, "ah jest about decided thet's the dangdest bunch of lies ary man ever told. Out all nat with cats up on a mountain and goosin' donkeys. One thang sort of bothers me, though. He did have thet thirty dollars an' ah shore don't know where he'd git thet kand of money unless he was tellin' the truth."

We didn't know whether to laugh or cry. Ruthie was deadly serious and she looked mean enough to blast any man with a twelve-gauge shotgun. One of the women, a timber operator's wife, spoke up. "Don't worry, Ruthie," she said. "He's probably telling the truth. What he did

was put a cable on the tractor and hooked it to a sta-
tionary engine and pulled it down. The engine's called a
donkey in the woods. You won't have to worry until he
comes home and tells you he's late because the whistle
punk got sick and the crummies had to wait for the pond
monkeys. Then you'll have something to think about."
(I never did figure that one out completely, but I'm told
it means the man at the whistle became ill and forgot to
blow the end-of-the-day signal. Naturally, the pond monkeys, the fellows slipping from log to log in the mill pond,
were late getting to the jalopies which take them in and
out of the woods. The crummies, in a word.)

Ruthie was a constant delight, with her sharp mixture
of ignorance and peppery mother wit. I remember a time
we were driving to Eugene and passed a sign advertising
the wonders of a new community: WE HAVE NATURAL
GAS. Ruthie read it aloud. "Ah, gawd, kid," she said,
"ain't thet somethang? Ah got thet netural gas, too, but ah
an't braggin' about it." Ruthie was a gold mine for me
when I started writing a column, "The Oregon Corner,"
for *Popular Ceramics*. I was always sure of getting dozens
of letters whenever I included a Ruthie story. A reader
complained once that my column sounded as though it
had been written at the last possible minute (as it is) and
worried a bit about my syntax and spelling. I read the letter to Ruthie. "Why, hale, Gladys," Ruthie said, "you jest
tell thet ol' gal she's lak an ol' maid who finally gits a man.
She better take you jest as you are, 'cause she an't lakly
to git no better." Ruthie was fascinated by my writing
and even tried a little herself when she saw me at the type-

writer. She'd puzzle over her work and rarely showed it to me. "Say, kid," she began one day, "how'd you spell rat?"

"R-a-t," I said.

"Aw, no," Ruthie said, "ah don' mean mousie rat, ah mean *rat*, lak *rat now*."

She returned from a Los Angeles holiday, once, with a tale of her experiences on the freeways. "Ah gawd, kid, you jest wouldn' believe thet place an' the number of cahs there is on them roads," she reported. "Ah always thought ah was pretty smort, but ah shore got messed up down there. Finally, ah jest had to stop an' puzzle thangs out. Well, kid, you'd have thought ah was trying to stort enother wor the way ever'body started honkin' at me. There must've been a hundred cahs honkin' at me an' swervin' aroun' an' people hollerin'. Then a guy comes by slow an' hollers, 'Hey, you, Oregon. What the hale do you thank yore doin'?' He talked jest lak one of our loggers an' ah lakked thet. 'Don' get your pants in an uproar, frind,' ah said. 'Ah'm jest studyin' where ah'm at.' 'Why the hale don' you jest git offen the freeway?' he hollered, an' ah said, 'Freeway? Ah gawd, effen ah knowed this was a freeway, ah'd ruther paid a little an' stayed offen the gahdam thang.'"

Shawn, our Park Avenue poacher, was even more puzzling to Ruthie than the Los Angeles traffic. Shawn was an oddity in our valley, quite beautiful, fragile, sophisticated, used to the chatter of *Le Pavillon* and 21, puzzled and a little resentful of the harsh life of the Oregon woods. Shawn ("Now where in hale you suppose she got thet name?" demanded Ruthie) joined the Drain gang in ce-

152

ramics class. After Shawn's arrival we got very little ceramics done. The girls were fascinated with Shawn and she took over the class time with tales of high and low life in Manhattan. *Ceramics for Fun* sometimes meant very little ceramics.

Shawn talked freely of her life in New York. She had been a private secretary with an admirable arrangement with her wealthy boss: daytimes, she was a comfort to him with her efficient shorthand and typing; nights, she comforted him in the Park Avenue apartment he provided. It was a dandy arrangement, marred only by the presence of an unreasonable wife just over the horizon. So unreasonable did this lady become, in fact, that it was thought advisable for Shawn to take a brief vacation. She chose Seattle for her exile, and there she met a towering, handsome, brawny tree topper in town for Lumber Week. They did the town, and at the end of a week they were married. "Tomorrow we're going home," the logger told Shawn and she beamed; ah, to be carried over the threshold of her own home in those sinewy arms! They arrived at the logger's cabin late at night, and early the next morning the groom awakened Shawn. "Wha . . . What's the matter?" she cried. "It's still dark."

"Get up and get breakfast," said the man. "I've got to get to work." Shawn slipped out of bed and into maribou mules and a blue chiffon negligee.

"What in hell do you think you're dressed for?" the logger asked.

"Why, breakfast, silly," smiled Shawn.

"Okay," he replied. "First thing go down to the creek and get a bucket of water." Shawn said she cried steadily for the first four days and then she settled down to be a dutiful and efficient wife. The ceramics girls were divided. Ruthie and her blonde friend, Dorothy, thought Shawn should have gone back to her millionaire on Park Avenue and throttled the unreasonable wife. The rest of them, except for a very religious girl who regarded Shawn as a miserable sinner, figured she was lucky to get a good logging man.

When Shawn began to study religion (she suddenly concluded that her Park Avenue days made her a bad, bad girl), the class was split again. Ruthie was outraged. "Effen thet Shawn gits ackin' so gahdam holy aroun' here, she won' tell us them good New York stories," she complained. The religious girl was pleased with Shawn's new bent, but thought her aim was bad. For Shawn sought out the occult and the unusual in religion. "Truth is beauty and beauty is truth," she told us. "I am trying to obtain a union of my soul with the universal Oneness. *Om mani padme hum*—Om, the jewel is in the lotus." Ruthie looked at Shawn as though she had gone mad. "The lotus symbolizes the Universal Being and the jewel is the individuality of the speaker," Shawn declared. She spent hours sitting cross-legged in her mountain cabin, concentrating on Absolute Goodness, Truth, and Spiritual Essence. "It's an ancient Hindu philosophy, called yoga," she explained.

At the next meeting, Ruthie's friend Dorothy showed up with a towel turbanned around her head and a long, flowing red garment. She sat cross-legged and "charmed" a cobra she had made out of a black stocking. Ruthie then went into a trance. "Oh, man, paddle me home," she moaned. "Ah got yogurt! Ah'm gittin' mahself in union with a mess of sour cream." Shawn was furious for a moment but the new-found peace of yoga stayed her hand. "Truth is beauty," she chanted while we all howled. "One day you will achieve understanding."

Ever since Pappy and I were married, we have had a pot of coffee on the stove and anyone who dropped in was welcome to help himself. Naturally, we carried this happy custom into the valley with us and, over the years, an amazing number and variety of people have come to know about it. Fishermen from the river come in to sip coffee and lie about their luck. Truck drivers frequently stop to have their lunches with us. "I heard about this place on the coast down in California," one truck driver told us. When the ceramics classes began, we had a twelve cup percolator. It was not big enough and we soon acquired two more. Ever since, those three pots have been turning out coffee in a never-ending stream.

The coffee was just a come-on for real eating when the ceramics business really got under way. The mudhens (the classic name for ladies who dabble in ceramic clay) came to class simply laden with food. It got so I hardly ever had to cook a meal. None of the eating was planned but the girls always brought something with them. Sometimes it would be casseroles of macaroni and cheese, venison roasts and pies of various kinds; in berry season we could always expect two or three blueberry pies and sweet moist strawberries with cream so thick you could cut it. In salmon season, we had salmon. On one memorable oc-

155

casion, a class of seven showed up and every last one of them had brought green peas and nothing else.

The mudhens were much more than casual students; many of them became fast friends and we had frequent parties for them, usually pot luck. I remember trying to contact Ruthie to invite her to an impromptu party. I could not reach her, but I got a neighbor. "Tell her to bring all the mudhens she can find," I told him. Ruthie appeared at the party bearing a cake and a basket covered with a dish cloth. "What's that?" I asked. "Ah don' know," Ruthie said. "Thet Mr. Adams nex' door tol' me to brang it." Inside was a dozen old river mudhens, neatly dressed. No one ever eats mudhens and I've wondered what Mr. Adams must think of our cuisine.

Every ceramics class engendered new tasks. Soon, I was asked to speak and give demonstrations throughout the state. Making speeches was good for business and I enjoyed meeting and talking to new people and interesting them in the art of ceramics. I kept up a constant line of chatter at these demonstrations, filling in the periods when we had to wait for a glaze to dry with tales of the valley—and Ruthie. Ruthie got to be quite famous and sometimes she went with me when I made these out-of-the-valley appearances.

Once in a while, someone in the audience (from what motive I know not) rises to challenge me. This never bothers me because I've never posed as an artist: all I claim to be is a sound teacher and I've often said most of my students turn out to be better ceramists than I. Ruthie was with me when a persistent lady took me on. "You know what I've heard about you?" she asked querulously.

"No telling," I replied.

"Well, I heard you're going around telling everybody about ceramics and that you don't know any more about it than a hog knows about holy water." I started to reply, but Ruthie was on her feet in an instant.

"Why you got yore nerve talking to the teacher lak thet," she said. "Here she come all this way to learn you a little somethang an' you got to git up an' exercise yore jaw." She turned to the audience. "Don't pay her no mand," she said. "Her mouth an't no prayer book, even effen it does open and shet."

Thet took care of thet.

❧ ❧ 9 ❧ ❧

Happy Birthday,
Dear Scottsburg

I DON'T REMEMBER exactly when I first felt that I had
become a part of the valley. Those things just creep up
on you, anyway, until you suddenly find it hard to believe
that you ever could have lived any place else. But if I *had*
to pick a time when that feeling first made itself felt as
real and deep and abiding, I'd have to name the day
Emma Hedden put on the biggest show in Scottsburg's
history. "Emma's Centennial," folks around here still call
it.

There had been talk around the valley for several weeks
that Emma was about to propose a celebration of Scottsburg's hundredth anniversary. We all thought it would be
a community picnic, a get-together for the old-timers.
None of us were prepared for what she had in mind when
she appeared at a special meeting of the Grange.

Emma didn't even go to the front of the hall to speak.
She just stood in front of her chair, dressed in the white

blouse and black skirt she usually wears in the store, with her hair wound up on top of her head and her hands folded in front of her. "I guess you all know why I'm here and I don't think any of you want to hear a lecture from me," she said. "But I do want you to see this plan." She unrolled a very large piece of paper and handed it around. We saw it was a map of Scottsburg. We looked at it in silence. On it she had marked the things we would need for the centennial: place where visiting dignitaries will sit; cooking area; speakers' platform; marshaling ground for parade; facilities for press; posts for highway patrolmen; space for picnic tables. "We've got to have a covered area where the old folks can sit," Emma said. "I'm not going to have them sitting out all day in the sun."

"Maybe there won't be any sun," someone suggested—not entirely off the beam since the Oregon sky always freights clouds and we get over seventy inches of rain a year.

"There'll be sun," Emma said placidly.

She had cryptic notes and marks all the way down to the Grange Hall and beyond. Someone asked, "What's that you've got marked down here at the Grange Hall, Emma?"

"We're going to have rest rooms there," she replied, "and we'll put in some couches, too, because somebody might feel faint in all the big crowd."

From the rear of the room came a derisive shout. "Some crowd! All fifty of us!"

Emma snorted. "Well, if that's the attitude you're going to take, we might as well give up the damn thing right

160

now. We'll have fifteen hundred people here or know the reason why."

Fifteen hundred people! I had a feeling of physical shock. Thode Andrews' head wagged back and forth. Maggie Burton started from her chair. Men turned toward one another and whistled soundlessly and their eyes got big. The women smiled nervously. Emma took no notice of the rustling which swept the meeting. "Jane Murphy is going to be co-chairman with me," she announced. She turned to Annie Attaway, whose husband had just died. "I can't think of a better thing for you than some work," she said. "Annie, you and Margaret Goodwin, Mae Van Natta and Winnie Albro will work directly under Jane as her assistants. I'll tell you what to do later."

Earl Harris stood up. "I notice there'll be a speakers' stand and picnic tables and covered place for the cooking," he said. "Would you like me to take over getting the lumber we'll need?"

Emma replied, "Well, Earl, I've got something else for you to do. E. K. Wood and the Long Bell Lumber Company have got lumber and I don't see any reason in the world why they can't supply all the wood we'll need."

"Why don't you ask for volunteers to help with the building?" asked Thode Andrews. That was a mistake.

"Why don't you wait until I tell you all the things I've got on my list?" Emma snapped. "I'm going to need all you men. Forget the lumber and the building. I'll get the lumber companies to take care of that."

Emma ticked off her items. A large sign to be strung across the highway between Pop Smith's gas station and

161

the pool hall. "The Mobilgas people will do that," she said. Bob and John Thomas to arrange for the parade entries. Walter Palmer in charge of floats (although we doubted he'd have much work to do). She turned to Dorothy Palmer. "I want you to write up all this stuff and the history of Scottsburg for the newspapers," she said.

"Oh, Emma, I'm no writer—" Dorothy began.

"Well, it's time you learned," said Emma. "You've got a good education and you ought to be ashamed of yourself if you can't write. I want all the stories on the front pages of the papers."

Lucy Riley, Maude Applegate, Ida Wessela and Helen Read were named to supervise all the cooking. "While I'm talking," said Emma, "you girls figure what you'll need by the way of stoves and roasters and coffee makers. I'll get them from the Douglas Electric Company. And you'd better figure on maybe a couple hundred more than fifteen hundred people so we'll be sure to have enough." Every time she mentioned fifteen hundred people, everyone's heart skipped a beat; at least mine did. I think everyone in the room was a little dazed at the magnitude of Emma's plan.

As if we had not been shocked enough, Emma turned toward Mary Levenhagen, the official valley invalid. "Mary, for I don't know how many years, you've been coming to the Grange and you never have taken an active part," Emma said. "Now, you're going to be in charge of the pioneer exhibits. I want you to clean out my store window and fill it with all kinds of pioneer relics. You get on the phone—" this gave us a chance to lose some of our nervousness in laughter, since we all knew Mary was never

162

off the phone "—and find out what stuff everybody has. I want you to do it yourself." Emma paused a moment. "I want you to go over to Bill Burchard and get that baby Bain wagon the Burchards rode across the plains because we'll need that for the parade."

Mary Levenhagen spoke up in a hopeless voice. "Oh, Emma, I don't think they ever let that wagon out."

"Don't talk like that," Emma replied. "Just get the wagon. This is the anniversary, and if that damn wagon falls to pieces, well, it's served its purpose. It's lasted a hundred years and that's long enough."

I was laughing inside at the idea of Mary Levenhagen having a job to do when I heard my name. "Gladys, are you going to see Annie Kruse soon?" I nodded. Then Emma said, "No, never mind. I better tend to her myself. I'll get her to represent the Applegates who came to Oregon about the time Scottsburg started." (Emma never admits the Applegates got to Oregon ahead of the Heddens.) "What I want you to do is get enough salmon to feed fifteen hundred people."

I felt my face get hot. "Where?" I wailed.

"If I knew where to get it, I'd get it myself," Emma said matter-of-factly.

The rest of the meeting is something of a blur. I couldn't think of anything but salmon. If everyone ate eight ounces —and I knew men, and women, too, who could eat two pounds at a sitting—that would mean 750 pounds of salmon. Where would I ever get such a mountain of salmon? I was still struggling with my problem when the meeting ended. Jimmy Van Natta came up. "Don't worry, Gladys," he said, winking. "All you have to do is go down to Reedsport and buy a few jars of salmon eggs. Then get yourself a couple of old settin' salmon and let them hatch out the eggs for you. You got no problem."

When the time came, I went to Old Man Heyes's fish wharf at Reedsport. "How much salmon will I need to feed fifteen hundred people?" I asked.

"You mean fifty people?"

"No," I insisted. "It's for Emma's centennial. She says there'll be fifteen hundred people to feed."

"Well, if Emma says fifteen hundred, we better get salmon," Old Man Heyes said, "but I wouldn't have predicted we'd have fifteen hundred people until hell froze over." Then he told me what to do. "Go down to Winchester Bay, which is about the best salmon fishing spot in the world, and tell them what you want. Only one thing: make sure the guy is sitting down because when you tell him you want a thousand pounds of salmon, he's liable to fall over."

Two days before the centennial, everything Emma had ordained had come to pass. Everyone had given and done everything she had ordered—and more, they did their work with a flourish. A speakers' stand edged out into the highway; the cooking area, with a dozen stoves especially connected by the power company, was in place and a three-sided counter was ready for serving. The gasoline company's big sign hung from the gas station to the pool hall. "Scottsburg's 100th Birthday," it read. "Welcome." A covered area for the aged was ready and chairs had been gathered from Reedsport and Coos Bay. "I want chairs," Emma had said. "Benches aren't comfortable for old folks." The loudspeaker system, donated and installed by Jack Unger, the Reedsport undertaker, had been tested. Pies and cakes were ready for the ovens. There was nothing to do but await the great day. For Emma's sake, we all hoped somebody would show up for the party.

An hour before the parade was to start, the sun shone confidently. By nine in the morning, Emma's checkers had counted eighteen hundred people packed into the narrow canyon where the few houses of Scottsburg stand. They were jammed from the turn in the highway clear down to Paul Wessela's house a half mile down the road. Al Flegel, the mayor of Roseburg, the county seat, arrived with all the officials of Douglas county, with a band and a float and five tremendous birthday cakes. Newspapermen from Reedsport, Drain, Eugene and even Portland, along with photographers, ranged through the crowd.

The highway patrol blocked the road above and below town and allowed only a few cars at a time to pass through. The speakers' stand, brave in red, white and blue bunting and fir boughs, stood half way across the highway so the traffic *had* to be one way. (Pappy had spotted the "misplaced" speakers' stand early in the game. "You can't block the highway like that," he told Emma. "*You* can't," she said. "I can. Anyway, it's got to be where it is to make room for the audience.") Old-timers dressed in pioneer clothes crowded the chairs of the covered area. We all climbed the porch of Hedden's store to look at the window full of old cooking utensils, the ox yokes, tiny, old-fashioned spectacles, dresses a hundred years old, the lights of the river steamer *Eva*, tools and jewelry, coffee grinders, a boot jack, axes and shoes, old newspapers and books.

165

People streamed into town. They had to park their cars as far as a mile away. There were cheers when Uncle Ralph Stearns, who was ninety-eight years old, arrived. "You're crazy to make the trip," his doctor warned him. But Uncle Ralph laughed and said, "Oh, go away with you, boy. When my old friend Cyrus Hedden's granddaughter is having something like this, I can't let her down." He was too frail to leave his car, but it was parked in the shade and he spent all day talking to his friends and the youngsters who gathered around to hear how it was in the old days. Old Arthur Mack, the last of the stage drivers, was there, too.

And Ken Murphy was there. Ken was dreadfully ill and not expected to live but he insisted on attending Emma's centennial. "If it's the last thing I ever do, I'm going," he said. "Emma Hedden helped me when we first arrived in the valley and I just feel if I couldn't go to her party, the biggest thing in her life, why I wouldn't even be fit to die." He was carried to the Grange Hall on a stretcher and his doctor and a nurse stood by his side all day.

At precisely ten o'clock, the clear notes of a bugle soared through the town as a Boy Scout sounded the call the pioneers had used to break camp and signal the start of another day on the trail. And then, around the curve of the highway, the music of bands began and the Reedsport Boy Scouts, carrying flags, marched smartly into view. A tremendous cheer sprang from the smiling crowd. Behind the Scouts came a band, lashing out with "Oh! Susannah," and then came Emma Hedden, proud and handsome, riding a white horse and beaming at her friends. She wore a

166

billowing white piqué dress of the pioneers with a sun-bonnet to match.

That parade was everything a parade should be. It was handmade by the participants and you could feel the hearts and hands of the valley people in it. It was gay and funny and heart-moving, a memory-provoking spectacle (and I was crying to beat the band). Everything was exactly as it should have been: the old-timers cheered, kids whistled and ran along with the floats; dogs barked and the chickens that usually scratched the ground in front of the Community Church with a worldly air ran screeching for shelter. A pig, that was supposed to be *in* the parade dashed in and out of the crowd and ladies squealed. The band from Gardiner came by slowly on a float of deep green fir boughs and a funny fellow from Reedsport, dressed in a high-button coat and top hat, walked along bowing and making faces at the crowd.

"Mexican" muleteers drove their mules along the highway, making the beasts jingle along to their high-pitched cries of "huppah! huppah!" and "mulah!"—the same cries which once echoed through the lonely forest trails. The Levenhagens from Elkton and Drain had built an ambitious float depicting the Umpqua Indians as they lived before Levi Scott founded the town.

There were covered wagons with sun-bonneted passengers, and men in flannel shirts and peg-top trousers tucked into their trail boots. Young Norman, his face almost hidden behind a black and flowing mustache, a pillow under his plaid shirt, ground out "O Sole Mio" on a hand organ and led little Pinky Spence on a string. Norman depicted an old Italian who had wandered into

167

Scottsburg in the early days with his organ and a performing monkey. We'd all tried to find a real monkey but we finally had to settle for Pinky dressed in a monkey suit. Pinky was a bigger hit than a real monkey ever could have been.

There was an old man with a shovel and pick and gold pan on a burro to commemorate the days when Scottsburg was a supply center for the mines. A modern log truck, loaded with fir logs forty feet long, rolled slowly by. Gardiner sent a lovely float representing a social evening of the early days. Great-great-grandmother Elizabeth Sawyer's organ, which had come across the continent from Boston a hundred years before, was the center of this one. The men wore top hats and dress suits and the ladies wore bustled finery as they all gathered around the old organ to sing. Maggie Burton and Thode Andrews rode on the Grange float which represented Harvest time, Thode swinging an old hand flail and having the time of his life.

Roseburg had a float and so did Coos Bay and Reedsport. The barbershop quartet from Reedsport, all dressed up in pioneer finery and wearing top hats and beards, sang "When You and I Were Young, Maggie," as they marched, stopping from time to time to serenade special groups of onlookers. One float reminded us of the pioneers who had passed away and another, the "Old Friends" float, commemorated the pioneers who were still with us. The two couples on this float, Artie and Bertie Smith and George and Annie Kirkland, both had passed their fiftieth wedding anniversaries and they drew a huge roar from the crowd. The band from Roseburg tootled by and the

168

crowd began to sing the familiar airs it played. Finally, the wondrous parade was over and the spectators turned to one another to compare impressions and to tell which floats they liked the best. There was a short, pleasant lull and we heard the clanging of the old steamer bell on the river. As many as could ran down to the Umpqua in time to see the arrival of a replica of the original sailing vessel which once linked Scottsburg to the coast—this one filled with flowers and decked with pennants.

The highway patrolmen kept the highway clear and let the traffic, which had been held up for an hour and a half for the parade (an hour and a half parade in Scottsburg!) go on its way. Many people stopped their cars a short way up the road and came back to join our fun. Emma's schedule said the speeches would start at noon, and, on the dot, she arose on the speakers' platform, a small white figure and, as the crowd quieted, she raised her hands and opened the ceremonies with a prayer. Then we all sang "The Star Spangled Banner" and settled back for the speeches. The main address was given by Stephen A. Chadwick, grandson of Scottsburg's first postmaster, who later became Oregon's fifth governor. "I never had such a tough time making a speech in my life," he said later. "I kept smelling that wonderful food cooking—all those pies and cakes and turkeys and salmon—and I just couldn't keep my mind on what I was saying."

It was a fine speech. Stephen Chadwick spoke magically of the beginnings of Oregon, of John McLaughlin and the Hudson's Bay Company, of Marcus Whitman and his tragic end, of Levi Scott who was with the Applegate brothers when they pushed through the route of the

Old South Road, of the daring and far-ranging men who searched the forests and found the likely places for settlement and the routes for the wagons. In his speech and in the others, I re-lived Cyrus Hedden's heroic wandering along the misty, unfriendly coast. (Somehow, the words echoed the tone of my own Papa's voice as he told me the tales long ago.)

"Can you think of anything more dramatic than the meeting of Cyrus Hedden and L. L. Williams?" one of the speakers asked. "Both men, part of a company of twelve, were ambushed by screaming, blood-thirsty Indians near where the town of Bandon now stands. Six of the party were killed in the sudden, savage battle. The other six, all bearing marks of the fight, separated and dashed into the forest for safety. One of them was Williams, so badly wounded it was a miracle he escaped. We can see him now, his head split open to the bone by an ax blow, covered with blood, carrying a war arrow and a jagged arrow shaft in his belly, as he struggled through the forest. At last, he collapses at the foot of a tree, sinking down among the ferns. With his throat burning, his legs bare because he had lost his trousers in the melee, he lies in the moist ferns and waits for death.

"Then, by a wonderful coincidence, Cyrus Hedden, pounding through the forest ahead of the Indians, stops for a moment to rest. He hears a strange, guttural sound. We can see him leap behind a tree and listen. Did the Indians make that noise? Were they surrounding him? The noise is repeated again and again and Cyrus Hedden peers cautiously from his tree. He sees his comrade in arms, Williams, still as death, lying in his own blood. The odd

170

animal noise is caused by Williams' gurgling breath. In the dark and dripping forest, unarmed and surrounded by unknown dangers from animals and Indians, Cyrus Hedden bent to his task. He lifted Williams to his feet and guided him deeper into the woods.

"By all rights, Williams should have died. It is not too much to say Williams lived simply because Cyrus Hedden would not let him die. Half carrying, half dragging his fevered, delirious mate, Cyrus Hedden struggled for eight days to reach the Umpqua, a trip he could have made in a single day if he had abandoned his comrade. They made their way to the river and they must have presented a ghastly sight. Hedden without a shirt because he had given it to an Indian who helped him cross Coos Bay, Williams, weak, bearded, weakly calling for a death which would not come. Both men almost as thin as skeletons.

"Few success stories have beginnings as dangerous as this. And yet both men stayed in the Umpqua Valley and prospered. Cyrus Hedden first plied the blacksmith's trade and then entered the mercantile business. Williams, fully recovered after a few painful years, went on to become the treasurer of Umpqua County and served as chief clerk of the United States Land Office. He lived until 1880, a man rich in material goods and richer in friendships. The store Cyrus Hedden operated prospered; it dealt in every kind of merchandise from threshing machines to diaper pins. Gold dust was accepted as legal tender there. Mule trains and, later, wagon trains were outfitted at Hedden's store for the long trek to the mines. The store was a gathering place for the village, a place where tall

171

tales, some of them true, were told around the big black stove. Cyrus married Margaret Sawyers in 1854 and of their four children, two survived. One was Hulda Hedden who later became Mrs. J. A. Freyer. The other was John M. Hedden, the second white boy born in Scottsburg. When he reached manhood, he joined his father in managing the store. John Hedden, a hearty and humorous man, a beloved man, lived until 1941. And today, his daughter, Emma Hedden, maintains the Hedden Store over yonder, the oldest commercial establishment in Oregon under one management. The store you see here today is a monument not only to the spirit and courage of the pioneers but also to the integrity and faith of a strong family." I looked at Emma as she sat under her sunbonnet gazing straight ahead, a look of eagle pride in her eyes. Mom Kruse, listening to the fulsome praise of the Hedden pioneers, looked grim. But, then, as I said, Mom always looked a *little* grim. (She has a wonderful sense of humor, though, whenever some unexpected hilarity penetrates the grimness. I remember one day in Yoncalla when Mom said she thought she'd better call home and see if the new hired girl was doing her work, "or if the boys are in the kitchen flusterin' her." The new girl was from somewhere out of the deep South and spoke with a very broad accent. When Mom demanded to know what she'd been doing, the harassed girl drawled over the phone, "Ah jest started a fahr." At least, that's what she meant to say. Unhappily, she got the *f* in front of the *arted* and the *st* in front of the *ahr*, so her sentence took on a sudden, cosmic significance. After two minutes of laughing, Mom's face was a nice shade of purple.)

172

Pappy told me I looked as though I were in a trance. Other speakers recounted the origins of Scottsburg, first called Scottsville by Levi Scott, the tanner turned pathfinder. They told how the town had grown to become the metropolis of southern Oregon, and how the lower town was later flung downstream in a disastrous flood. The whole thing was summed up in an historical marker unveiled as a special feature of the centennial.

"Few Oregon communities," the marker says, "have had a more colorful history than Scottsburg. It was named for Levi Scott, a pioneer of 1844, who homesteaded here and founded the town in 1850. There was a lower town at the head of tidewater of the Umpqua River which became the site of business houses and mills. A mile upstream was the upper town, the distributing and shipping point for the mining regions and communities of southern Oregon. As many as 500 pack animals could be seen loading here at one time. The decline of the community began with the opening of ports nearer the market points in southern Oregon and northern California and the railroad building farther inland. In December, 1861, a great flood wiped out the lower town. Here, in 1854, was published the first newspaper in southern Oregon, the Umpqua *Weekly Gazette.*"

One by one the old-timers were introduced and applauded. Then, Frank Grubbe from Yoncalla led us all in community singing while fiddlers sent the melody flying from their strings. We all sang "Happy Birthday, Dear Scottsburg," and "Oh! Susannah," "Wagon Wheels," "Twilight on the Trail," "Trees" and the other old songs. And all the time we edged closer and closer to the spot where the food was cooking and sending out mouth-watering aromas. Then someone called, "Come and get it," and we all surged toward the counters where a dozen women lifted the huge platters of turkey and salmon and ladled out big helpings of salad and home-made rolls. (Roy Lewis, his mouth liberally smeared with lipstick and his eyes dripping mascara, was behind the counter, in a Mother Hubbard and sunbonnet. "They're going to need at least one strong arm in that kitchen," Roy said, "and darned if I'm going to be the only man in *that* crowd." So he put on a woman's costume and worked like a horse all day, stopping only to answer the gibes of his friends or to renew his lipstick.)

When it seemed everyone had eaten twice as much as he could hold, Jane Murphy, dressed in a flowered dress with lace petticoats and a blue sunbonnet, and Emma cut the six-story cake sent by the National Bank of Reedsport and the five cakes donated by Roseburg businessmen and county officials. And we ate some more. As the warm afternoon wore on, all of us wandered from group to group, renewing old acquaintances and talked to people we had not seen for months. The nicest thing was that the kitchen was not closed. It was just like at home after a big meal—if you felt you could handle just a bit more cake and coffee, it was right there for you. Even the hollow children were finally stuffed and sat under the myrtlewood trees, quietly gazing off into space.

The long shadows began to edge across the river and inched over the store and finally clear across the highway, and the whole narrow canyon was in the shade. When the sun went down, there was a coolness in the air and some of the old folks put on sweaters and coats and started for home. But Scottsburg that day was a hard place to leave. Al Flegel, the mayor of Roseburg, kept saying, "I've got to go. I've got an important meeting tonight," but he could not seem to tear himself away. It was the same with Stephen Chadwick, who had to drive to Seattle. He must have started to leave a dozen times but it was after dark before he actually got away.

10

Handy Man to Have Around

IT'S HARD for me to believe Rock Freyer and Gard Sagaberd are dead. Even today, when I go to Hedden's store in Scottsburg, I somehow expect to hear Gard's plaintive, private whistling and see Rock sawing Emma's wood. Rock was stooped and very thin and he wouldn't wear his false teeth between meals, so his mouth had a wide, happy, caved-in look. Gard Sagaberd was about five feet nine, built on the square, and as solid as the rock of Gibraltar. He had a black and white look about him: his hair and beard were very dark and he had the blackest eyes I've ever seen—eyes which could look right through you. Gard boomed out whatever he had to say, gesturing grandly with his big hands to help the words along; Rock spoke so softly you often missed what he was saying.

Gard picked up the mail for Emma's post office each morning and then opened the store for her. About the time

Gard reached the store, Rock would drive up in his Model T Ford and carry in the day's wood for the big round stove. If anyone came in, they'd wait on him: they were in charge until Emma crossed the highway and took over as mistress of the store. Rock and Gard did not talk much; they had said everything there was to say years before, but they puttered about the store happily, Gard usually whistling some quiet melody all his own.

That was the way it was the day "all those women got after Gard." Three large black cars stopped in front of the store and six or eight women and two or three little girls poured out and flowed into the store like some unexpected flood. "One minute the store was empty and the next there were people in every corner," Gard said. Curious people. The women wore long, full skirts of startling yellows and greens and pinks and their hair was covered with bandanas of blue and orange. They were dark and wore round gold earrings and every time Rock or Gard tried to wait on them, they'd grab their hands and start reading their palms.

"I see gold—money for you," the ladies cried. "You veel be reech." Gard (who believed a man can catch matrimony by contact) kept snatching his hand away, only to have another lady grab it and peer into his palm. "A long life and a happy one," cried the gypsies.

Rock and Gard kept backing and filling as women clutched at their hands and other ladies swirled around the store. The little girls, dressed in every way like their elders, darted in and out behind the counters. "You veel take an ocean voyage," cried the palm readers. "You veel meet a stranger."

178

"You let go my hand," shouted Gard. "You stop that."

"I swear I saw that one over there stick a can of peaches under her skirt," Rock shouted as loudly as he could. He streaked across the store after the miscreant, who ducked behind the ladies' underwear counter, upsetting a box of pink rayon panties. Gard wrenched his hand away from the palmist and yelled, "You stay away from me, you hear?"

Suddenly the gypsies were seized by a kind of frenzy of stealing. They lost all their guile and stole openly and without discrimination. They were bent on pillage. One flipped around and around a counter, with Gard in lumbering pursuit, snatching up three-dollar watches, lighter fluid, Christmas cards, rubber balls and costume jewelry. Another ambitious lady staggered toward the door under an enormous armful of black Levis and hickory shirts. Gard was distracted from his chase by a lady stuffing nylon stockings down the front of her dress and he leaped toward her. Rock cornered the peach thief who outweighed him fifty pounds and reached out for the capture. She intercepted his thrust and turned his palm over. "You veel be reech," she shrieked. "I see much good luck. Let go of me, you son of a beech."

Gard shook the nylon thief until her teeth rattled. "You ought to be ashamed," he roared. "Get those stockings out of your boosom."

The store was a gaudy whirl of yellow, red and green, curses and screams, pounding feet and the sharp clatter of tin cans falling from the shelves. The floor shuddered. The whole store shook. The telephone began to ring. Into this mad tarantella stepped Emma Hedden. She grabbed the busty nylon girl who tried to squeeze past her at the door. "Just what the hell's going on here?" Emma shouted in her reedy voice. One of the gypsy women reached behind the row of postal boxes and picked up a twenty-dollar bill. Emma let go of the nylon girl and hurled herself at the postal thief. "Oh, you goddam gyppies," she shouted, her tongue tripping in her anger. "Give me that money. That's government money." Emma wrestled the gypsy to the floor. Gard caught another and turned her upside down. Cans of vegetables, boxes of raisins, snuff, coffee and cigarettes rattled to the floor. She broke from Gard's grip and crawled toward the front door cursing in Romany. Emma had one hand on the twenty-dollar bill and with her other clawed great pieces of gypsy hair. "Give me the government money," she said between clenched teeth. Gard leaped over and pried the gypsy's hand away from the bill. Emma released her grip on the girl. The gypsy flock screamed from the store and into the cars.

In the sudden silence, Emma looked at the twenty-dollar bill, which was torn into three pieces. She looked at the groceries on the floor and the merchandise spilling out of boxes and at a stack of plaid mackinaws tilted precariously toward the door. "Goddam gypsies," she said. "After this, damn it, don't let any gypsies come in here, you understand?"

"Yes'm," said Gard.

"Yes'm," said Rock.

Later, polishing his communiqué of the gypsy battle for general circulation in the valley, Rock Freyer observed, "I thought sure Gard was going to faint when that gypsy lady took ahold of his hand. That's only the second time in all his life a woman almost got him." I asked about the first time. "It was a peculiar thing," Rock said. "A nice-looking lady come up here from California and she just about fell in love with the valley. She took one look at Gard and just about fell in love with him, too, I guess. She set right out after Gard. Well, Gard's as timid as a baby deer where single ladies are concerned, so he just disappeared. After a while she left the valley and we didn't hear anything more until Emma got a letter saying this lady had died and that it was her last wish to have her ashes scattered on the hill up by the cemetery. And a couple of days later, along comes a package and it was the lady's ashes in a little tin box. Well, when it came time to close the store, Emma sort of fiddled around and hemmed and hawed. Finally, she said it didn't seem right to leave a lady in a tin can in the post office over night. You could tell she didn't want to take it home with her. So Gard said, 'Put her in my car and I'll take her home with me and tomorrow I'll spread her around the hill.' Well, that's what he did and that's the only time a woman ever got a chance to spend the night at Gard's house."

As long as they could steer clear of gypsies, Rock Freyer and Gard Sagaberd were an efficient pair, able to meet just about any situation the valley could offer. One cold, miserable day I went to Hedden's store for stamps. It had rained for weeks, I had a dreadful toothache and, all in all, it was one of the few times I felt like taking off for a warmer climate. Rock and Gard were in the back of the stove with their chairs tilted and their feet on the rail of the big stove.

"You ought to put something over your head when you go out in the rain, Gladys," said Gard. "How come you never use an umbrella or a hat?"

"I don't like to be bothered," I said. "Anyway, today I don't care. I've got the worst toothache I ever had and I can't get in to see a dentist until Thursday. I'll die first."

"Does it hurt clear up to your eye where you're rubbing?" asked Gard, putting on a professional manner.

"It hurts all over the side of my head," I replied. "I can't tell just where." Rock Freyer looked at Gard. They nodded in agreement.

"We can fix you up," Rock said. "Gard, you get the nitre. I'll get the other." Rock left the store and Gard went behind a counter and rummaged in a drawer. He came back with a small piece of wet cotton. "Stick this in the tooth, if you can," he said.

In a moment Rock came in with some straggly-looking leaves. He did something to them behind the counter and then laid a damp mass on my aching face. "You just sit there and read your mail and we'll have you fixed up in no time," he said. I didn't know what kind of magic they were working, but in a few minutes the pain was gone.

"That's wonderful," I said. "What do I do if the pain comes back?"

"We'll show you," Gard said. He spoke to Emma and came back with a sheaf of paper. "These are the remedies the pioneers used coming across the plains when there were no doctors around," he said. "They seem to work real good." Below the date, 1838, I read: "Many of these prescriptions given here are original, the others are culled from the works and practice of the best physicians of both continents.

"For despondency—take a swallow of vinegar.

"Turpentine, in doses of twenty or thirty minims, will not only remove a headache but produce, in a wonderful manner, a soothing influence.

"Eye water—for inflamed eyes, use the juice of the strawberry after being strained and settled.

"A tea made of chestnut leaves and drunk in the place of water is said to have cured many obstinate cases of dropsy.

"The very simple remedy of common salt has cured many cases of fever and ague. A teaspoonful taken in water and a teaspoonful deposited inside each stocking next to the foot, as the chill is coming on; this comprises the whole of the treatment."

I don't know about those, but this is the one that worked on me: "Toothache—if the cavity is so great as to allow the air to reach the nerve, get some spirits of nitre and mix with alum; saturate a little cotton with it and apply to the cavity. If the pain extends upward toward the eye, or takes the form of neuralgia, procure some horse-radish leaves, take out the stems, wet them and apply on the face over the pain. This will generally bring relief."

Outside the valley, I've never heard of another community lucky enough to have a Gard Sagaberd. Whenever an unpleasant job had to be done, Gard volunteered. It got to be that we all expected Gard would do the small, onerous tasks. He did them cheerfully, whistling his soft little tunes, and he never expected payment, or, really, thanks. He belonged to the whole valley and I've never known another man who was so loved. I don't know how old Gard was, but he must have been very old. He used to visit our ceramics classes and, while he was always polite, you could tell he wasn't too impressed with our modern methods. "I used to watch the Umpqua Indians work up their pottery," Gard said. "They squeezed berries for color and even had some kind of a bug they squeezed and used the juice to make a green color. They didn't take nearly as much time as you gals, and they got some real pretty things, too." He delighted in talking about his days in the woods when long strings of oxen skidded the logs to the mill pond or the river. He worked in the woods many years and then became captain of *Eva,* the old steamer, that used to run the river between Gardiner and Scottsburg. Then, after *Eva* made her last trip, Gard came ashore and set himself up as the handyman of the valley. He did not do big things—although some of his deeds were formidable—but he was always there when something had to be done. When Emma Hedden was sick, Gard nursed her and cooked her meals and cleaned her house. When her favorite dog was ill, he took it to the veterinarian three times a week.

Gard was always matter-of-fact about his helpful acts; he didn't see anything special about his role. I remember one night the party line rang frantically and I lifted the receiver in time to hear a nearly-hysterical woman shouting, "My baby's just drunk lye. I think she's going to die." Then I heard Gard's voice: "Give her a cup of vinegar," he said calmly, "and I'll be right over." Or the time a young couple's home 'way back in the hills burned. Gard did not waste any time commiserating. He borrowed a pony and made the long trip, carrying blankets and pots and pans and food staples. "I don't know whether they need anything," he said, "but I guess we ought to see, just in case." Once, when we were away, a lineman was electrocuted and the electric current dropped so that the motors of the valley refrigerators and deep freezes could scarcely turn over, and, unless turned off, would burn out. Gard remembered we were away, let himself into our house with a passkey, and turned off our motors.

Gard Sagaberd knew everything there was to know about the valley, so when I was appointed to buy the turkeys for the Grange Thanksgiving party, I went to him. "Go on up to Arthur Mack's," he said. "He's got the best turkeys in the valley. It's a long way, but it will be worth it. He's the last of the old stage drivers and he can tell you a lot of stories about this country." Gard gave me a set of convoluted directions and I finally reached Arthur Mack's cabin set in a mountain meadow far from the highway. The house was very old, just straight up and down unpainted boards with a big, unroofed platform for a porch. On the right side of the porch was an enormous woodshed, open to the platform. Hanging there were eight turkeys, all dressed out, and six cats meowing and trying to get at the birds, plus three tail-wagging dogs. I went through a kitchen with a hand pump at the sink, and a wood stove, and the most heavenly odor: bread was baking in the oven, and on the back of the stove a big pot of pear butter simmered in spicy splendor.

Arthur Mack, an old man with a shock of white hair, sat in the bedroom-living room, surrounded by magazines which littered a table and a big bed covered with a hand-made quilt of many colors. "I heard about you new people," he said. "I'm glad you came." He wanted to talk and I wanted to listen so we spent a happy two hours. He told me tales of the days before the automobile, when Scottsburg was on the stage road between Portland and Sacramento. Thirty-five drivers worked the line, driving stage coaches and stage wagons and five hundred horses were stabled on the way. "I was the youngest stage driver of them all," Arthur Mack laughed, "and I outlasted all of them, too."

He told me one short tale I've always treasured. "For a long time," said Arthur Mack, "there was only one darning needle in the valley. It belonged to Grandma Drain. She was mighty generous with it and the people who borrowed it always made sure it got back to her. Well, one day, a little boy was sent to return the needle to Grandma Drain but he got to fooling around, picking blackberries on the way, until a bear came along and scared him off. When he got to Grandma Drain's, darned if he hadn't lost the needle. To show you how important it was, they closed the lumber mill at Drain and turned all the men out to look for that needle. The boy was so upset and scared he couldn't show them where he'd been, and at the end of the day the needle was still missing. That was one of the saddest days ever in the valley. A few days later a pack peddler came through for the first time, and when he heard about the lost needle he gave every lady in the valley a needle of her own. He was the most popular peddler you ever saw and some say that was the start of his good luck, for not long after that he opened a store in Portland that is still there today."

I was having such a warm time, I entirely forgot that the Merry Matrons of the Grange were having luncheon at my house. When I thought of it, I leaped to my feet and rushed outside. "Goodby," I shouted. "I'll be back to hear some more." On the porch there were now four huge turkeys, but these were *alive*. Arthur Mack's daughter nodded and said, "These are yours."

"But . . . but," I sputtered. "They're alive. I sort of had in mind some nice *dead* turkeys." There wasn't time to argue so we lifted the birds, legs bound tightly, into the back seat of the car. The turkeys looked at me with distaste and the car lurched down the road in a flurry of dust; with luck I could get home before the first guests arrived. We hadn't gone far when I heard rustlings in the back seat and I realized the turkeys were holding some sort of private convocation. Sure as shooting, they were plotting against me, but I couldn't break their code.

"Glark Gable," I distinctly heard one say.

"Whaaaat?" I cried.

"Goblet goblin gamma globulin," rumbled another. Then, louder, "Jack Jack Jackie Gleason."

The fourth chimed in: "George? George? George? Gobel Gobel Gobel." The turkey talk was swelling in volume, but I was busy with the winding road and could do nothing about the insurgents in the back seat. "Greer Greer Greer Garson," the turkeys yammered. "Grable Gable Gobel and Garson." Then, without warning, the insurrection began. There was a great whooshing

187

of wings and a thirty-pound turkey flopped willy-nilly into the front seat, fetching me a stunning blow on the head on the way. I braked the car furiously and came to a skidding, dizzy stop. The turkey on the front seat glared at me. "Greta Garbo," it rasped.

I quickly rolled up the window to prevent a mass escape and surveyed the scene. One turkey in the co-pilot's seat, three in back; all had escaped their leg bindings; all regarded me with chilling, beady eyes. "Shoo," I said to my co-pilot. "Go. Get out. Move." I nudged him and he clumsily hopped over the back of the seat. I followed him, why I'll never know, and found myself over my head in turkeys, screaming, flapping, dusty, panicked turkeys.

Next time you see a turkey, examine the leg: it is solid muscle; on the end of the leg is a set of splayed-out toes covered with a sort of imitation alligator skin; at the end of each toe is a long talon. The turkeys did not welcome me to the back seat; they beat their powerful wings in my face, leaped into the air, fell into my lap, sunk their talons into my thigh, and all the while carried on a maniacal chatter: "Gable Gobel Gobel Gobel." A sharp toe caught my blouse and ripped it from collar to waist. A wing smashed against my nose. I countered with a sharp left to the craw and took two rights to the jaw, a left and another right to the button. I got in a good left to the wattle but I was clearly outclassed and outnumbered. I grimly climbed over into the front seat, panting a little and muttering my views about turkeys. I was in tatters, afraid and alone on a desolate mountain road twenty miles from home—and luncheon guests were expected in twenty minutes. I started the engine. If the turkeys would just stay in the back seat, all would be well. Very gingerly, I started the car. I could hear the turkeys gloating over their victory, but my flailing around back there must have instilled some respect because, for the rest of the way home, the birds maintained an almost phlegmatic calm. It wasn't until I turned into our driveway that the turkeys began to chatter again. "Geep Going," one of them said as I turned. He sounded just like Edward G. Robinson.

Gard Sagaberd did so many things in the valley that his one truly heroic feat was almost taken for granted. It started, as did so many things in the valley, with the party line. We could always tell when something was wrong because the telephone bell took on a rasping edge of urgency. I was not surprised, when I put the receiver to my ear, to hear a jumble of excited voices. "Gard Sagaberd's the only one near."—"I don't see how he can get to the river through all those blackberries."—"Does he have a boat?" I could not make out what the trouble was, but a neighbor, running toward her car with blankets over her arm, shouted: "Three people fell into the river by the summer bridge."

Little by little, I pieced the story together. Just at dusk, a one-armed man and his wife and daughter, trolling in the river, had somehow overturned their boat. The accident was seen from the opposite shore and someone hit the party line. Gard heard the call: the boat had tipped over directly below his house. But between Gard's house and the river a solid mass of blackberry brambles covered the seventy-foot slope to the stream. Gard, although he was badly crippled with arthritis, covered his face with his gnarled hands and somehow slithered, pushed and ripped his way to the river and plunged in to reach a struggling figure in the channel. Pulling through the water with his strong arms, Gard quickly reached the woman and pulled her to shore where he left her draped over a rock. He scanned the water and plunged in again, swimming powerfully toward the man. The desperate fellow, flailing about with his one arm, was almost ready to give up when Gard clamped a hand on the back of his collar and dragged him to shore.

By this time, boats had arrived from the other side of the river and people in cars were humming up the road above Gard's position. Someone started a fire and the rescued pair were covered with blankets and given coffee. "The doctor's coming," someone said. Gard stepped into a boat and joined the search for the still-missing girl. It was dark and the fire sent its orange reflection to the water when Gard returned, wet and almost freezing. Someone handed him dry clothes and he changed in the shadows. We all waited quietly, the only sound the muted putter of the outboard motors on the slowly moving boats patrolling the river. Flashlights struck green beams in curious patterns as the boats criss-crossed the channel.

A doctor arrived and the rescued couple were lifted into cars and sent to the hospital. There was nothing to do but listen to the drone of the motors and wait. Then there was a shout from the river and the motors speeded up as the boats converged on a point near the summer bridge. We could see the boats heading for the fire on the beach and watched as the men lifted a limp form from the lead boat.

190

Gently, they laid the girl on the narrow strip of sandy beach and began artificial respiration. Strong men worked until they were exhausted. They worked over the girl three hours before they finally admitted defeat. Then, quietly, we all went home.

"Poor little girl," said Gard. "They found her in three feet of water. If she'd just known it, she could have stood up and wouldn't have drowned."

Although Gard was on the party line almost as much as his sister, Mary Levenhagen, it was not until his death that we learned just how ardent a listener he was. He was fascinated by long distance calls and telegrams; on the wall next to his phone was a large chart where he had transcribed many telegrams and conversations, with comment. "This guy thinks he's a city slicker, but Workman's not so dumb."—"I don't know how Gladys talks so fresh to those big city guys. I guess she just talks that way to everybody." Pinned to the wall was a note, bearing the name of a local family: "They don't get many calls. Remember to call them sometime." To a note about another family buying a sheep, he'd appended: "Wonder what they want so much mutton for?"

Gard was another of the unsuspected poets of the valley. He was a man who always lived close to the river and the woods and the weather. Twice I had a glimpse of the way he felt about it. One overcast day, when the gray clouds were very low and seemed to be rolling and tumbling just over our heads, Gard watched as the clouds parted for an instant and let a shaft of strong sunlight through. "I've lived here all my life," he said, "watching those clouds. I think they roll away like that once in a while just to let us know the sun is still up there. That way we never lose track of the sun." And one day, a bright day, Gard and I stood watching the river.

"You ever have a yen for diamonds, Gladys?" he asked.

"No," I said, "somehow I've never cared much for jewelry."

"Well, if you did," he continued, "you'd never find as many as you can see right here on the river. Just look at them sparkle as they roll down to the ocean. You'd think they'd be lost forever, but the sun draws them up and soon the diamonds are back in the river again for us to watch."

Gard's special charge was the community cemetery which stood on the hill a few hundred yards east of our house. I'd see Gard's car turn into the cemetery road almost every day and I knew he was checking "his" property. The cemetery is not large, about two hundred by three hundred feet, and is surrounded by a wire fence and entered through whitewashed gates on the upper edge. It is on a hill and slopes gently. At the upper end are eight or ten firs and at the lower border, just before the hill falls away steeply, there are oaks and masses of Scotch broom. A few small maples and yellow-green shrubs are inside the enclosure. Most of the headstones are weathered now. Most of the graves have tin cans or glass jars to hold flowers and some of them are enclosed by light, unadorned wrought iron railings which look like children's playpens. For half a century, Gard dug the graves in the dull golden soil. For fifty years, Gard put back the earth over the caskets and mounted the headstones. (Gard worried a bit about the modern, polished-granite stones which the latest graves have. "I just wonder if the old-timers would like them," he said.) There is no grass but Gard always had the weeds under control and stopped the blackberries at the fence. The cemetery was an oasis of quiet, carved out of the forest, a place where "repose" had full meaning.

When Gard caught a bad cold, all of us in the valley felt a premonition of his death. At the store or the Grange, we did not speak of his cold: we thought of the way he had aged since his heroic rescue in the river. Gard never spoke of the rescue; instead, and rarely, he would speak quietly of the girl who had drowned. Although no man could blame himself for that, Gard was oppressed by his "failure" to reach the girl in time. He shook his head. "She was in only three feet of water," he said. "She didn't have to die." After the rescue, you could see his arthritis and rheumatism getting worse as every day tightened the screws in his aching joints.

He had to give up some of the things which he considered his normal duties. A few days before his death, he told Emma Hedden, "There's only one worry I've got left and that's about the cemetery. I'm getting to the point where I won't be able to dig graves any more and I'd sure hate to turn down a friend."

Gard's bad cold turned into pneumonia and in a few days he was dead. The valley understands death, but his was different. I think our first feeling was that we had been cheated; he was ours and should not have been taken away. Emma Hedden wept; the first time I had ever seen that strong woman taking comfort in tears. For many days, tears would start to her eyes whenever Gard's name was mentioned. (She was not too overcome, however, to insist that Old Abe must get a new pair of pants for the funeral.)

The day before the funeral, I saw Norman Wetherly and his brother, Floyd, tramping through the snow, carrying picks and shovels. They were going to the cemetery to dig Gard's grave: the first time in fifty years that Gard himself had not been at the end of the shovel. The funeral was held at the Grange Hall. That was fitting because Gard was a charter member of the Grange and had been its first master. Besides, the community church was not large enough for the people who crowded into Scottsburg to say goodby to Gard Sagaberd.

At about two in the afternoon, I heard cars arriving for the ceremony at the graveside. It was snowing very gently and every noise was muffled. There was a quietness over the valley. I was not the only one who spoke in whispers. Everyone parked their cars on the highway because we all knew the curving, climbing road to the cemetery would soon be impassable if cars churned up the ruts. The mourners walked up the hill and I remember looking at the valley in its winter beauty: over all was white and powdery snow, covering the familiar fields and the dark trees. The valley looked as though it had been decorated for a bride.

The sky was dark and overcast in contrast to the bright whiteness underfoot. Gard's friends gathered around the open grave. Back of them the sharp trunks of burned trees were silhouetted against the gray sky, and masses of flowers made great gashes of color against the snow. There were more flowers than any of us had ever seen at a valley funeral—more even than in summer, when everyone had garden flowers. Everyone was dressed heavily: the men in boots and mackinaws and the women in long coats, galoshes and bandanas on their heads. The Reverend Parker, of the Episcopal Church in Gardiner, opened the ceremony with a quiet prayer, and then Marjory Grubbe sang "In the Garden," one of Gard's favorite songs. As she sang, the weak winter sun broke through the clouds. The sun sent up tiny splinters of light from the snow crystals and Thode Andrews said it for everyone: "Look at that," he said. "Isn't that exactly the way it should be for Gard? I don't know of anyone who liked the winter sun more than he did. He just loved the winter sun." And then a curious thing happened and you could feel it sweep through the crowd: the funeral was no longer a sad and doleful thing; Gard's friends suddenly realized how lucky they had been to know Gard Sagaberd and, instead of gloom, there was a certain happiness among the people at the graveside.

Howard Hinsdale stepped forward after the song. The Hinsdales have been on the river ever since white men arrived on the Umpqua and Gard had been captain of their sternwheeler, *Eva*. Now Howard Hinsdale said: "This moment was made for Gard Sagaberd. It is like his very life—simple and real and with a golden glow which reached down into every heart in the valley. Speaking for the Hinsdales, we feel we have lost not only a faithful and trusted employee but a man who was a personal friend to each and every one of us." The Reverend Parker spoke what was in our hearts, too: "We are not losing this

195

humble man. We are only sending him on ahead to brighten the way for the rest of us. Gard Sagaberd can never really be gone from this valley. As long as people inhabit this land, they will hear the story of a good and untiring man who went among his relatives and friends doing good and asking only friendship in return."

As the Reverend Parker spoke, a cowbell gently accented his words. Bartleys' cow and four or five sheep nudged their way through the snow-covered Scotch broom and stood solemnly at the fence, facing the grave, watching and listening quietly.

Then Marjory Grubbe sang a hymn, and Gard's friends began to leave the cemetery. As they left, they joined in with Marjory. Their breath was white and steamy as they sang the familiar words: "So I'll cherish the old rugged cross, till my trophies at last I lay down; I will cling to the old rugged cross and exchange it someday for a crown."

I can still see the long column of Gard's friends walking slowly down the hill from the cemetery, with the mist of their breath white against the white of the snow. I can still hear their muted voices as they sang the day we buried Gard Sagaberd under the snow.

11

The Fire Beast
Comes

Umpqua summer is soft and warm. The light takes on an effervescent quality which delights the eye and, in the summer, the clouds pile up gold and white castles high, high above the silent fir forests. The rains come infrequently in the summer months and the Umpqua itself gradually recedes from its high water mark; finally, in years of little summer rain, long ridges of rocks skim above the water and the river grasses growing in clumps on the rocks make whole stretches of the river look like Japanese flower arrangements.

But when there is too little rain the summer is a time of peril. Then the forest bakes out in the constant sun and the dry air sucks out the stored waters of the wet winter and spring. The forest becomes a vast oven, filled with the odors of pitch and gums, the resins which need only a spark to explode into ripping, racing flame. During that summer we'll never forget, the fire weather chart in Forest Service stations pointed ominously to red: the humidity dropped and the whistles in a dozen canyons signaled the men out of the woods: it was too dangerous to work in the tinder-wood forest, triggered for a fire. Forest Service lookouts high in their towers felt the tenseness, and their eyes roved the lush green carpet of trees below, peering out for smoke they hoped they would not see. Foresters moved tautly around their stations, knowing the smallest spark—a backfire from a truck, a spark from a cigarette, the erratic lightning—might start a conflagration in the explosive forest.

Then, in a moment of frightful carelessness, a logger, impatient to get along with the building of a logging road far back in the Smith River wilderness, set off a dynamite blast. In an instant, the silent forest was churned into a tornado of sound; the blast rumbled through the files of trees and clattered boulders against the forest. When the roar of the explosion died, there was a new sound: the curious, ominous whoosh of fire clambering through the foliage of fir trees. With a curse, the loggers turned their cats against the ground fire, but, within a few minutes, turned and fled from the crackling, roaring, racing monster in the woods. The fire sent a mushroom cloud towering into the barren sky and the lookouts from forty miles around shouted the news into their telephones and radios: "We got a big one on our hands."

All of this seemed remote to us, snug on the bank of the Umpqua, at least a dozen miles from the blaze. When we saw the sudden spurt of smoke in the air, it was just something to be commented on and wondered about; we felt no urgency, no unease. "Looks like a forest fire over there," we said. "Yeah, a big one." But the timber men knew better. E. K. Wood and Long Bell and independent timber operators like Harold Wooley at Drain knew the signs and started all their cats and jeeps, trucks and men toward the base of the smoke which began to smudge a growing section of the sky. If we could have seen the actuality of the malignant force chewing into the forest we might have been a bit uneasy, but it was too far removed; someone would put out the fire in a day or so, we were certain.

A day or two after the fire started, we had left the valley for a few hours and returned just at sunset. As we emerged from the highway tunnel near Elkton, I gasped at the overwhelming sunset clinging to the hills and then, with a numbing shock, I realized no sunset could be where I looked. It was the Smith River fire, still many miles away, but close enough for us to feel physical shock as we watched the gigantic arms of flame embrace and destroy the forest before our eyes. The valley was hazy with smoke; we could smell it and we looked toward the main smoke a dozen times a day, wondering when the fire fighters would control it. But there was no real cause for worry, we told ourselves. Bone-tired, beaten men who had fought the fire stopped in for coffee, but they could not describe its horrors; they did not have the words, and their eyes looked flat and far away as they recalled the fantastic power of the fiery beast in the forest. "We had a pretty good fire line in all along the ridge," they said, "but the fire just blew up and jumped the line like it wasn't there." When the fire ran, the sweat-streaked men could do nothing; no power on earth could stop the rampaging, cannonading terror: then it was a matter of trying to save men and machines. The fire "crowned"—the flames leaped from top to top of the trees in an unstoppable aerial conflagration; in a few moments, five thousand acres of forest were blackened. The terrible forces involved created their own weather: vicious updrafts sucked in local winds to whet the fury of the blaze. These capricious winds flung howitzer blasts of flame and burning bark which soared far ahead of the main fire and spotted new islands of flame in the forest.

The fire was still far away but the smoke lay in a stifling cloud in the valley; a rain of fine white ashes began to fall and at night the sky was neon red under the canopy of smoke. For the first time, we began to look at one another as though there was a chance the fire would not be stopped. I looked carefully at our immediate terrain and was comforted. Our own land ran north of the highway through daffodil fields and then the forest began; but the forest was at least a half mile from us. The house stood in a clump of regal firs, and below the house, rolling down to the river, were masses of blackberry bushes, willow and alder. If these ever caught fire—but, no! no fire could span the daffodil field. Or so I thought then, in my ignorance of what fire in the forest means.

The fall of ashes was constant, coating men, machines, the rooftops and the fields with a fine gray coat. Some of us wore handkerchiefs around our faces to keep the ashes out of nose and mouth. The fire, still beyond the mountain ridges, dominated everything in the valley. As long as the ashes fell and the smoke seeped among our trees and

streamered out over the river, there could be no thought
of normal pursuits. People began to talk in whispers. We
rarely took our eyes off the advancing, towering smoke
and, in moments of quiet, we could *hear* the fire gnawing
its way toward us. The constant rain of ashes turned the
grasses and trees gray, and we tracked the stuff in on
our shoes when we went in at night. Then we noticed, in
the pungent half-light, that our part of the valley was beginning to fill up with heavy equipment, lumbering water
tankers, smaller pumpers of Forest Service green. Overhead we heard the whirr of a helicopter above the smoke.
Caterpillar tractors on heavy trailers turned into our
daffodil field, jeeps and stake-sided trucks arrived and
men in hard hats marched out against the enemy. We had
not wanted to admit it before, now there could be no escape. Our front yard was going to be a front line.

The fire was so close that at night the towering flames
lifted high above "our" ridge, the last mountain between
the fire and the river. Our house was brightly, flicker-
ingly lit with a garish light from the flames and when we
awoke at night—as we did frequently—the walls glowed
frighteningly and we could hear the fearful cannonading as the juices of the trees exploded. Frightened deer
plunged down the steep slope of our mountain and
dashed into the open field and stood near the firefighters.
Some of them had great burned patches on their soft
brown pelts, and I thought of the thousands of animals
and birds that must have perished in the rampaging
flames. A venerable black bear waddled down from the
mountain during the night and took up temporary quar-

ters near the creek that runs down our property into the Umpqua. From time to time he would come out of the underbrush, look toward the smoke, and sniff, for all the world as though he was gauging the progress of the fire and making up his mind as to the best course. It did not seem a good omen when he slid down to the river one morning and swam across to disappear in the willows on the other side. Firefighters delivered to us two tiny fawns whose mother had been killed in the flames, and we fed them milk from a bottle. We watched a mother bear trying to persuade her cub to cross the Umpqua with her. The mother plunged from the bank, swam out a little way and turned to see if Junior was following. He was cowering on the bank. So the mother bear returned, gestured with her head toward the river as though she was giving orders, and plunged in again. Once again, the little one refused to enter the water. The mother returned to the bank and belted the cub across the ears and chopped his little rear end with a heavy paw. He bawled like a baby, but when his mother took to the river, he jumped in too, and swam manfully across.

Since our place stands at one of the widest spots in the valley, many people used our front yard as a vantage point to watch the fire. Shawn, the displaced Park Avenue girl, very pregnant, was there one afternoon. She had never seen nature on such a rampage and she was terrified. (She was not the only one.) Ruthie strode up to Shawn. "Where's yore man?" she asked.

"He's up there fighting that awful fire and I just know I won't ever see him again," wailed Shawn. "And I don't know how I can stand having his baby after he's gone."

Then she stiffened defensively. "Just what do you want with my husband?" she said icily.

"Don' you worry thet pretty little haid," said Ruthie. "Ah don' want nothin' to do with yore *HUSbind*. Mah man's got to know where he can find yore man rat away so he can git some cats up on the mountain an' bury some donkeys."

Shawn looked down wildly at a few of *our* cats which were mewing around her feet. Then she began to sob. "I don't think this is any time to joke about cats and burying donkeys," she cried.

Ruthie turned to the rest of us. "Ah swear ah never heard of sich iggorence," Ruthie said with scorn. "Why enny dang fool'd thank she'd know all about cats an' donkeys by now."

We were worried about our tinder-dry old house, nestled under the firs; we knew that a flying brand from the fire would turn the trees into torches and the house would go as fast as kindling. Pappy and the neighbors tried to rig a pump in the river to get water to the house, but, after laboring for more than a day, could not get it to work. And, every minute, the fire came closer. Now the forest just the other side of our mountain was ablaze and the skyline was alive with rockets and comets as the fire belched blazing bits of bark and luminous balls of fire over the ridge. As we watched, one of these blazing messengers soared a half mile over the ridge and landed, showering sparks in a tree near the cemetery. There was a sudden blossoming of fire in a tree top and the men in our field shouted, raced to their equipment, and roared up the cemetery road to do battle. The fire shot another comet over the ridge and another tree began to smoulder and flare, the underbrush caught fire, and, as we watched, *our* forest began to seethe with flame.

Now I was certain our house was doomed. If the fire could send out blazing scouts a mile ahead to start new fires, we could not expect our house to stand safely. I ran inside where Mama was making coffee and sandwiches for the firefighters. "You've got to get out of here now," I told her. "I'll take you over to the Kruse's for the night." But Mama would not hear of it. "You want me to leave and miss all the excitement," she said. "Then I'll have to spend the rest of my life listening to you tell me what happened. I'll stay and see it for myself."

We both went outside. Now the fire was burning fiercely on our mountain, burning up toward the ridge, toward the main fire, which still had not reached the crest. We could feel the stinging heat on our faces and the smoke swirled around us, kicking up great gusts of choking ashes. A chunk of flaming bark landed in a sputter of sparks within ten feet of us and we looked up apprehensively at the smoke covering. We could see streaks of orange tracers as the fire spit out blazing embers before it. As we watched, one of the comets fell into a fir tree on the Bartley place, a hundred yards down the road. The men watched it carefully and let out their breath as it seemed to die out. But, in an instant, a bit of flame no larger than a man's fist glittered in the dark foliage, another blazed just above it in the resinous needles, then another. Men started the engine of a pumper truck and sent a stream of water up the tree. Now, despite the smoke, we could see a pattern developing: the fire would soon reach the crest of our mountain and, very clearly, it seemed our beautiful land was destined to be wholly devastated.

The official word came a few minutes later. Wayne Read, who was directing the firefighters in our sector, came up to me. "The wind's coming up and there isn't a thing we can do about it," he said. "You better get some things together and get ready to move. I'd say you've got about an hour. And don't pack any more than you can carry in a suitcase."

An old refrain ticked through my mind: "When in trouble, when in doubt, run in circles, scream and shout." I'm a circler and a screamer from 'way back and I darted into the house and up the stairs to the attic where I kept my most cherished possession, a fur coat. I slipped it over my house dress and ran down stairs. Pappy grinned when he saw me. "Where are you going in that outfit?" he said. "You look pretty hot for August in this neighborhood." Reluctantly I laid the coat on the bed and looked around for the most valuable things in the house. There was a delicate glass wine set I loved. I wrapped it carefully in newspapers. Then I looked around at objects which had surrounded me for many years. I simply couldn't make up my mind which ones to take. On one of my dashes through the kitchen, I came upon Pappy. "What are you doing?" I asked waspishly.

"Eating," said Pappy.

"Aren't you going to pack?"

"All packed," said Pappy, reaching for another piece of toast. We finally got some things together and went out to the car, ready for the order to leave. But after a little while we looked at each other as the thought struck us simultaneously: we don't have to go; we just have to be ready.

There was a shout from nearby and a firefighter running by us said, "They've got the pump working." Soon a stream of water was sluicing over the roof, wetting down our home against the growing heat. The fire on our mountain was racing toward the ridge. Wayne Read gave us some hope. "If the fire on this side reaches the top at the same time as the fire coming up the other side, there's a chance they may kill each other off."

We watched as the flames whipped up the hill. Then, with a crash that sounded as though locomotives were colliding and grinding together, the two fires met at the top of the ridge. There was an overwhelming lashing of wind. Flames and smoke jetted and writhed into the sky over a half-mile front. Then, gradually, there was a slackening of pace and we could perceive that the fire was dying. It died slowly and reluctantly. In the trunks of trees, in a thousand hidden places, small clots of fire persisted for days: at night the stricken forest glowed with a baleful and eerie beauty as little twists of wind livened red coals. Our forest was a pincushion of blackened spires; all trace of green had been rubbed out in the cataclysm. The trees around the cemetery had burned and now the gravestones were in full sight from our yard. We looked out on a new world: wherever fire had been was a black smear across the land—and the ash lay two inches deep on the fields and blew sporadically along the highway. On the last day of the fire, slow rain began to fall and the heavy drops drilled little craters in the gray ash.

In other sections of the valley, the story was much the same. In some places the fire hurled outriders of flame across the river, but these fires were quickly subdued. In the valley itself the fire burned to the edge of the highway in many places before the saving rain arrived. Dr. Albro's barn was periled and almost burned—but not because the firefighters were not diligent. The good doctor is a camera nut and he was so intent on getting color slides of the flames as they approached his barn that he continually waved the fighters away. "Just one more shot," he cried, in the manner of photographers everywhere and, being extremely deaf, was unable to hear the firefighters shouting for him to get out of the way. "I think we ought to let the barn burn, too," said one of the men gruffly. "Then he could get some real good shots."

❧ ❧ 12 ❧ ❧

Lace Dolls and
a Little Bill

I DON'T SUPPOSE there's a chance I will be held personally
responsible for the acres of ceramic objects which
emerged from our kilns on the Umpqua and, indirectly,
from kilns all over Oregon. There would be no true jus-
tice in that! And yet, I sometimes have a disturbing
dream in which streams of ceramics, both Aphro- and
eru-dite, swarm from the kiln (like firemen from a Walt
Disney firehouse) and fly directly toward me with an
intent which seems evil. Elephants and donkeys, cats,
ash trays, puppies, wine kegs, lamp bases, ash trays, full
sets of elegant porcelain dinnerware, clocks, toby mugs,
vases, plaques, ash trays, Colt revolvers, nymphs naked
and clothed, nuns playing baseball, monks at bowling,
candy dishes, ash trays, dessert plates, letter boxes, tea
pots, ash trays and lace dolls.

Ah, yes, lace dolls!

When we first started, we were simple folk, satisfied to

take a flower apart and use its petals as a pattern for clay flowers which we laboriously stuck together, colored, and fired. We had to learn how to stick these flowers on vases or dishes or whatever we were making. The trick was to scrape down to the original clay and then attach the flower, but before we learned that, there were many heart-breaking failures. (I remember one gorgeous mistake, in which a sky blue iris slipped off a vase in the kiln and attached itself to a female figurine, right where the bustle would have been if she'd worn a bustle: it made an unusual bit of ceramics.) We'd try to put on a smooth glaze and get a wonderful crackle or crazed finish. When we wanted a crackle, it would come out smooth. Pack rats drove us crazy by sneaking in and dropping nuts and seeds into the molds and ruining them. We experimented with every kind of glaze I heard of, including Epsom salts. After that episode, I stopped in at the drug store at Reedsport. "That must have been some party you had at your place the other night, Gladys," said Mr. Burdick, the druggist. "Every last one of those ceramic ladies stopped in here for Epsom salts afterwards." I didn't try to explain.

But we kept on. Like drunkards, driven by a craving for demon rum, we caroused on and on, through figurines and miniatures, through elaborate molds forming elaborate drinking vessels and, finally, to lace dolls.

Perhaps you've seen these dainty and sometimes exquisite dolls, dressed in the fashion of Marie Antoinette and other fancy ladies of the fancy past. Meissen and Copenhagen have made them for many, many years but, until recently, no one in America knew the secret of firing their delicate laces in ceramic clay. When my mudhens reached a certain degree of sophistication, many of them wanted to make lace dolls. I went to Los Angeles where I picked up the latest word on the art. Gladys Burbank, my first teacher and a great experimenter, and others had fiddled around until they broke the secret of the laces: they found that real lace, when dipped in diluted ceramic clay, could be fired, whereupon the hardened ceramic clay looked exactly like the original material. What a discovery! Pretty soon, we were all playing dolls again, a thing, I suppose, no lady ever outgrows.

We'd make tiny dresses of various materials and hang these on an inverted cone of clay, stick on appropriate moulded heads and arms and, presto! a doll. We advanced from these to truly splendid dolls in Elizabethan and Louis XVI costumes with ruffs and piled-up hair. This was not as easy as it sounds, of course. The clothes and their laces had to be laid on with considerable care and there was always the danger of the whole thing collapsing of its own weight in wet clay.

I remember the time Mary Colley of Elkton spent three solid weeks making a dress for a sort of super lace doll. "Mary, you better not hang anything more on that doll," I warned. "You've got everything but the kitchen sink on it now and it's getting too wet to stand." But Mary has a very good mind of her own and kept adding certain touches she believed the doll required. Finally, the masterpiece was finished. As we all stood back in silent admiration, the magnificent doll, too exquisitely overloaded and too wet to stand the strain, very quietly and gently settled into a mass of mud—a mass of mud with a patrician head covered with curls and feathers in the middle.

Looking back on some of the things that happened, I no longer question the magic of this special mud. It has brought me cops and robbers, a broken neck, a thousand friends, and more deep pleasure than anything I've ever tackled. A visitor recently remarked how well equipped my kitchen is, adding, "I've never seen so many gadgets." I just smiled and said, "Ceramics."

It was late in the fall and I had arranged for the mudhens to leave the premises for a few weeks while we all recuperated after an intensive spell of work. Someone had the happy idea of inviting everyone who had worked at the house to a party in my honor.

I was pleased as could be—but on the morning of the party I dragged myself out of bed feeling hot and cold and dizzy. A doctor who dropped by in mid-morning (doctors show up at our house about like milkmen at other homes) told me I had a pretty good temperature and should stay in bed. "Nonsense," I said. "I'm fine. I could take a little thing like this party standing on my head." Being a diplomatic fellow, the doctor said nothing and left. As a matter of fact, I did feel pretty good until the first of the mudhens arrived: then I discovered I was very dizzy indeed and just wished they would all go away. I stood still while the kitchen whizzed around me and when things rocked back into place, I looked up to see a fubsy little fellow, dressed all in black. He poked his head in the kitchen door and said, "Where shall I put these?" gesturing with two black satchels about the size of a doctor's kitbag. "Put them anywhere you like," I said woozily. The kitchen was beginning to spin again and I was in no mood to bandy words with little men I'd never seen before.

When I opened my eyes, the little man in black was there again leering at me. This time he had two large suitcases. I closed my eyes. A few moments later there he was again, staggering under the load of a huge bag. "The doctor was right," I thought. "I'm delirious . . . little men in black . . . bags that grow." I tottered into the living room. Spread over the tables and chairs and even on top of the big stove were terribly gleaming knives, hundreds of knives. There were shining pots and pans and pails but mostly knives—paring knives, steak knives, butcher knives, carving knives, skinning knives, berry corers, cheese cutters and for all I know, machetes, cutlasses, scimitars, sabers and snickersnees. With what wit I had left, I managed to pass out.

The doctor was with me when I woke up. "I told you you should have stayed in bed yesterday," he said. "Now you're in the hospital and I'm going to make sure you stay down for a while." Ruthie and her blonde friend Dorothy were standing by my bed. I gestured feebly toward them. "Are you real?" I asked.

Ruthie snorted, "Ah an't no reasonable facsamile."

"Then let me ask one question," I said. "Was there a little man there with bags that got bigger and a lot of knives or am I crazy?"

"Ah, gawd, kid, you ain't crazy," said Ruthie. "Thet little man was the Stanley man, the one thet comes around to sell pots an' pans an' all thet kind of thang. He was supposed to go to Pansy Andrews's place for a Stanley pahty an' when he saw all them cahs in yore front yahd, he figured he had the rat place. So he come in an' jest laid out his stuff. About thet time you give a scream an' keel over an' lak to scared us to death. Ever'one felt so sorry for you, goin' to the hospital an' not staying for yore own pahty thet we jest about bought ever'thang thet Stanley man had. Ah, gawd, kid, when you git home you all'll have the dangdest collection of knives an' thangs thet you ever did see. We bought you so dang much stuff and win so dang many prizes, thet little man said he'd throw in Mr. Stanley himself as a bonus."

One night, while I was sitting in the workroom of the studio, I heard someone enter. Pappy and Norman had gone to check the motor of the bulb cooler and when I heard the door open, I called, "Is that you honey?" There was no answer, so I called again.

"Naw, this ain't honey," someone answered. I walked into the sales room. A young man of about twenty-two was standing under the light. He wore a plaid shirt, well-worn jeans, and heavy shoes. His face was bronzed and his eyes were deep in their sockets. His left hand fumbled at something in his pocket. I'll never know why, but instead of saying, "Hello," I said, "Come on in by the fire, where it's warm." He didn't answer. "What are you doing out in this weather without a coat?" I asked. "I didn't hear a car. Are you walking?"

"You ask a hell of a lot of questions, lady," he said nastily, just as the party line phone jangled our ring. "What do you say we don't answer that," the boy said. I was frightened. My stomach flipped over, very fast, at least three times. The phone rang again. "Look," I said, "if I don't answer that phone there'll be neighbors here in two minutes wanting to know why. That's the kind of neighborhood this is. They know I'm alone and they'll expect me to answer." He raised his chin toward the phone and I lifted the receiver. It was Maude Applegate saying she and Paul would be right down to pick out a vase for a gift. I told the boy they were coming. "Go on over to the house while they're here," I said. "There's some ham in the ice box. Make yourself a sandwich." He looked puzzled for a moment as he considered what to do.

"What's the pitch?" he said. "How do you know I won't rob you?"

I laughed. "We've got a rule around here that we always get half if anyone finds anything worth taking," I said, trying to be calm and clever at the same time. He saw lights turning into the driveway and disappeared. Paul and Maude stayed only a little while but as they left a truck driver wheeled into the yard and came in for coffee. When he was gone, I started to go to the house. "No need to go over there and see what I'm doing," said the boy from the back room. "I'm out here."

He came into the sales room. "Why didn't you tell those people I was here?" Suddenly I realized I had nothing to fear from this scared boy. "Why should I tell them anyone was here?" I replied. "You can see by now people drop in any old time. I would have sounded pretty silly saying *you* were here." There was a silence and I added, "Now, let's cut out all this foolishness and have a cup of coffee."

I poured and then went into the house for some cookies. When I came back, I asked, "What are you doing here?"

Just as though I had asked him the time of day, he replied, "I came here to rob you. I saw your men go up into the field and I knew you were alone."

I laughed. "Son, the next time you get that idea, don't ever rob a ceramics studio. We're the most broke people in the world."

"Then why are there so many of them?" he asked. I told him and when I start talking ceramics, I tend to ramble.

Pappy and Norman came in about midnight. "How about giving me a hand with these molds?" Norman asked the kid. The boy looked at me. "I'm going in the house and put on some milk for hot chocolate," I said.

I went to bed and worried a bit. I was almost certain the boy had a gun, but I was equally certain he'd never use it after our long talk. I debated whether to tell Pappy and Norman. And while I lay there wondering what to do, a wonderful thing happened: I opened my eyes and it was morning. When I went into the kitchen, the "robber" and Norman were having coffee. He did have a gun, I found out later that day. I bought it for ten dollars. If you ever want to see what it looked like, come on up to the Umpqua: I'll sell you a ceramic replica of it for a little less than ten dollars.

I don't suppose I have ever been as excited as I was the day I started for Los Angeles for my first ceramics hobby show. I had the back end of the car loaded with samples of my students' work and I was sure we would carry off all the blue ribbons. I made the first nine hundred miles all right but when I was within three miles of my destination, another car nudged mine and I woke up in a hospital. Or almost in a hospital. In accordance with the immutable laws of such places, they would not let me in until I had given my mother's maiden name, the number of petals on a daisy, my last three addresses and the depth of water at average mean tide in the Bay of Fundy. I didn't know any of the answers and my solution to the whole thing was simple: I went to sleep.

When I came to again I was not only in a hospital bed, but also in traction as the first step in remedying a broken neck. After a week or so with the weights, they let me use my arms again and Stella Hardy came over with some ceramic clay for me to play with. The Sisters were fascinated with my clay and soon I had a very responsive audience. Stella brought some paints and I finished up a few pieces which she fired for me.

One unexpected result of this was that the Sisters moved two despondent patients into my room as an experiment to discover if ceramics would lighten their load of misery. It worked. They became interested in ceramics and their interest spurred the Sisters to set up a therapy room for them and others. They had trouble locating a room for the ceramics classes I agreed to give, but finally everything was set and I was wheeled down into the basement for the first class. Since my neck was in a high brace, I couldn't see where we were working. All I could tell was that it was inconvenient because something obstructed the wheel chair under the table and I could not get very close to my work. The Sisters finally confessed: we were working in the hospital morgue, the only space they had been able to find. Whenever anyone died, the classes had to be postponed.

Out of that class with depressed patients, I got an insight into hobby ceramics which was to become the dominant theme in my work. But it was not tied down until a few months later when I returned to the valley, minus my neck brace. I was teaching a class in Roseburg, seventy-five miles from Scottsburg, when one of the women said, "This is so much fun we should call Clover." I asked who she was. "Oh, she's wonderful," they said. As a kind of afterthought they added: "She hasn't any legs and only one arm." Someone telephoned Clover Kerr and reported, "She's coming over with her mother."

I, of course, thought Clover's mother would steer her in in a wheel chair. But a few minutes later in walked a handsome brunette in her mid-thirties. She flipped off her coat and, in a matter of minutes, I could see Clover Kerr was cleverer than most of us, using just her left hand. Some people never do master the art of modeling a rose-bud in ceramic clay but Clover managed on the first try. She rolled the clay deftly between two fingers and that was the center of the bud. She stuck it on a pin, picked up a sharp tool and peeled off a bit of clay. By some magic I've never been able to duplicate, the clay that peeled off was a perfect petal for the rose. Another delicate slice with the tool and she had another petal, which she deftly rolled around the center. "I'm glad I spent that year in Arizona," Clover laughed.

"Why?" I asked.

"Well, the cowboys taught me to roll cigarettes with

my left hand and if you can do that, anything is simple," she said.

I often saw Clover after that and wondered just what we mean when we speak of handicapped people. True, Clover Kerr had been injured in an automobile-train collision; she wore artificial legs and she had only one arm. But she led a wonderfully full—not merely normal—life.

A few months after I met Clover, I met Aileen Lattin. Here, if ever, was a hopeless case: she was a polio victim, and when I first met her she had been completely paralyzed for fourteen years, so immobile that she could move only her head and shoulders. Yet this indomitable girl had taught herself to write by holding a pen in her mouth. We had brushes made with spatula-shaped handles and Aileen learned to paint ceramics. I gave Aileen lessons for a long time and every time I saw her I came away refreshed at the resiliency of her spirit. One night I said to Pappy, "I'm going to take Aileen down to the ceramics show in Los Angeles." Pappy did not say anything. "The poor girl's never had a chance to have a good time," I continued, expecting some opposition and getting my licks in as fast as I could, "and I think it would really make her happy. We could show some of her work and she'd have a chance to talk to other ceramists and feel a part of the world again. We'll have to take her nurse, but we can take the station wagon and put all Aileen's special gear in that."

"Sounds like a good idea," Pappy said.

We did take Aileen and her nurse to Los Angeles. She attracted a great deal of attention and, for a week, was feted like a queen at film studios, restaurants and night clubs. Few girls have ever had such a fling and Aileen was almost speechless in her delight; she polished the memory of that wonderful trip for the rest of her brief life: she died less than three years later.

Clover and Aileen were just the beginning of an enthralling new facet of ceramics: teaching the handicapped. Of course, my regular classes continued. The Workman *Ceramics for Fun* idea spread throughout the entire state. At one time, we were supplying two hundred ceramics studios! Most of them had been established by my former pupils. Business prospered; Pappy, who kept the books, astounded me when he told me we were doing a $40,000-a-year gross business. I was so busy, with my classes at home and traveling throughout the state, that I almost forgot we were also in the daffodil business.

When Pappy first started in as a bulb grower he followed the ways of the other growers in the valley. But he soon became discontented with the methods in use. He read everything he could find about daffodils. He traveled to other bulb-growing areas of Oregon and Washington to see how others were solving their problems. At first, bulb growing was almost wholly a matter of hard, hand labor. All the daffodils in the valley were planted by hand; women, working on their hands and knees, laboriously plopped each individual bulb in the row. They covered the bulbs as they went, scooping the rough dirt into the furrows. The more Pappy looked at this, the more he fretted. First, he did not like the idea of the grueling stoop labor; second, hand labor is expensive and he knew there had to be a better way.

When a bulb grower found that, by the use of double discs, bulbs could be covered mechanically, Pappy immediately put the idea to work in our fields; but the hand planting continued to nag at him. During the season, it seemed he could talk of little else: "There has to be a better way," he repeated. Then one night while he was reading, he gave a whoop. "By golly, I think this is the answer," he shouted. "Look at this." He handed me a farm journal and pointed to an ad. "Little Bill planting machine," it said, and there was a picture of a spraddled-out contraption with two hammocks swinging underneath. In the hammocks were two girls, taking plants from a hopper fed from above. They rode horizontally over the ground, planting with both hands as the machine trundled along under its own power, following the furrows.

Just as soon as Pappy could get financing, he had a Little Bill planter in the field across from the house, beginning the two years of experiments and modifications necessary to adapt Little Bill to daffodils and the Oregon soil. But in the end Little Bill worked, and became the wonder of the valley, indeed the wonder of all the bulb-growing areas of Oregon. Soon delegations of bulb growers were on hand to inspect and discuss the merits of Little Bill. Today there is probably not a single bulb planted in Oregon without aid from a Little Bill.

There was another stint of hands-and-knees labor at the end of the season when the daffodil bulbs must be dug from the ground. In the beginning, bulb growers attached a hand plow to a long chain back of a tractor and turned the bulbs out in a rather haphazard manner. Then someone improved on this by fixing the plow rigidly to the tractor—but the bulbs, turned out of the ground, still had to be picked up by hand. Pappy was one of the first to adapt a potato digger to this chore: now a mechanical digger rolls down the rows, lifts the bulbs up and into waiting boxes. Those two machines took much of the drudgery out of the business—and, incidentally, saved labor costs.

But if stoop labor and back-breaking customs irritated Pappy, the goofy marketing system of daffodil buds enraged him. Each grower had a favorite florist to whom he consigned all his flowers each year and each grower kept the name of his wholesaler a dark secret. Since the buds were sent on consignment, the grower never actually knew if he had made or lost money until the end of the hectic picking season. Then the word might come back: "The market was thin. We sold half of your buds and had to dump the others." There was no recourse for the grower. This seemed idiotic to Pappy and, as usual, he did something about it—which almost doubled his work. He went to Seattle and worked out details of a new system of marketing. There was one condition. "I can get you a better price than you have been getting," the broker told Pappy, "but I must have *all* the buds from the valley." Then it was up to Pappy to convince the other growers to join the marketing plan. The first year it was difficult, but when Pappy's group got up to six dollars more per thousand flowers than the "outsiders," the others were quick to join. (While Pappy handled the marketing of the valley's flowers, he was allowed exclusive use of the party line for two hours in the middle of the day to talk to brokers.)

In the lush soil of Oregon, daffodils increase mightily. The first year, you plant a single bulb and it puts out a single flower. But while it is in the ground, the bulb grows; the second year, the bulb might have two or three "noses" and each nose produces a flower. Then the newer parts "slab off" and begin a new bulb cycle. "You have to dig the bulbs at least every two years," Pappy says, "or they get smaller on you." Also, each year after the digging, there are always a few slabs and bulbs left in the field. Technically, they are known in the daffodil industry by the expressive if unusual name of "bastard." These must all be carefully removed to prevent random blooms from popping up all over the field.

A year or so ago, Pappy reviewed the bulb business. "I always thought if I got up to twelve or fifteen tons of bulbs, that would be a lot of daffodils," he said. "But this year we dug forty tons and left ten acres in the ground. We sold twenty tons of good bulbs and put back the other twenty so next year we'll have about a hundred tons and the year after that about a hundred and fifty. Daffodils are something like rabbits that way. The valley isn't big enough to hold that many more bulbs so I don't know what we're going to do. You're not supposed to throw them in the river, they're too hard to burn, and nothing will eat them."

(I did my part. I am an inveterate bidder for "mystery packages" at the Grange and soon after Pappy had outlined our possible inundation in bulbs, I confidently bid seven dollars for a Grange package. It was a hundred-pound box of bulbs Pappy had donated.)

The hectic time for bulb growers comes in mid-February when the daffodils begin to bud. Everyone rushes into the fields to snap off the flowers before the buds become too large for efficient shipping. When Pappy was marketing the bulbs for the valley, he would gather the whole day's pick and whoop them up to Drain to be shipped in refrigerated railroad cars. That was a time! Pappy and Norman would roar to Drain with the buds while I was rushing in the other direction to Emma's post office to get out shipments of ceramics supplies. In those days, the trick was to get the buds out of the valley as soon as possible, selling in dribs and drabs as the buds came to flower. Now the business has changed. "It's no longer a thing of selling a handful of buds here and a handful there," Pappy says. "We are likely to sell 500,000 buds at a crack to a big chain store." To hold the buds for an accumulation of this size, Pappy urged the growers to build coolers to keep the buds at low temperatures and delay their opening. Other growers held back, so Pappy built a cooler of his own, which has already demonstrated its worth. Other growers are now coming around to his view that coolers are needed to meet the changed market conditions. Pappy has been responsible for many major changes in the business of daffodils, and now finds himself one of the biggest growers in the valley. Last year we harvested a million golden blooms.

It isn't often a panhandler comes through the valley but a man stopped at our door one day when Ruthie was holding the fort. "I'm not a bum," he said, "but I've been walking almost all morning and I can't find a place to eat. I've got money and I can pay."

"You willin' to do a little work?" Ruthie asked and the man said he was. She handed him a shovel and pointed across the road to where several men were clearing bastard bulbs from the field. "Take this thang an' go over there an' git them bastards out of thet field."

"Ah, gawd, kid," she told me later, "when I rung thet dinner bell, this stranger was the only one thet showed up. Ah asked him where the others was at an' he said, 'Well, ma'am, you tol' me to git them bastards outten thet field an' I chased them dang near two miles up the road. Ah don' thank you'll have no more trouble with them.'"

13

Low Shoes, No Lipstick

GLADYS, do you know who went home today?" Pappy had been unusually silent during most of dinner and his abrupt question surprised me.

"No," I replied.

He told me. "They were here three days and you spent fifteen minutes with them. You didn't even eat with them and they came nine hundred miles to see us." Pappy shook his head. "I'm not blaming you," he continued, "but it just isn't like us. I was with them only about an hour myself."

The rest of dinner was a silent time. I realized suddenly I had not been to the Grange for over two years! A new family had moved in less than a hundred yards down the highway and I did not know the woman's first name! The only news of the valley came from the gossip of my mudhens. How long had it been since I had taken time for a neighborly, leisurely talk with anyone in the valley?

Ceramics for Fun had just about taken over my life.

When I was not teaching classes at home, I was gallivanting all over the State of Oregon. I enjoyed these classes and I enjoyed seeing the wonderful countryside, but this side of the business meant I was away from home a lot. Too much? Probably. And, for the last few years I had been getting busier every day. For ceramics had given a new twist to my life, an enjoyable twist: I was asked to act as mistress of ceremonies at the annual breakfast of ceramics suppliers and studio owners in Los Angeles. This was the biggest meeting of its kind on the Pacific Coast and I was flattered and flustered by the whole idea. It was a cinch: all I did was stand up and tell some of the tales of the valley, liberally interspersed with some of Ruthie's Arkansas slant on life. They were good enough to ask me to MC their breakfasts for several years; then the Idaho ceramists asked me to do the same job at *their* annual breakfast. People in Detroit and Chicago asked me to appear at their shows. I went to Chicago two and a half months before the ceramics show to speak at luncheon clubs, garden clubs and various other groups—I talked to anyone who would listen to the story of ceramics, and the valley. Chicago was the first show I worked for a fee.

With me away from home a good deal, Pappy and Norman had just about taken over the ceramics business. And it came to me very sharply they had not been on the river for steelhead or salmon for almost two years. They barely squeezed out a single day off to try to bag their bucks.

Whatever else it might have been, this was not why we had come to the Umpqua. We had worked hard at the business and it simply would not stop growing. (I don't

228

suppose we could have picked a worse spot in the whole United States if we had originally intended to make such a go of the ceramics business. I remember overhearing a conversation in a Los Angeles studio one day. A ceramics distributor was speaking: "I used to think I was about the biggest guy in this business," he said, "but I hear there's an old dame up in Oregon who sells twice as much stuff as I do." "What's her secret?" I asked. "Well, I don't know," he replied. "I hear she gets women from all over the hills and they just sit around gossiping about their husbands and babies and exchange recipes. They say she doesn't know anything about ceramics but she sure has somebody fooled.")

I thought of my engrossing work with the mentally ill and handicapped people and what a joy ceramics had been to so many of them. I thought of my local students, the kindly people who had transformed my life in the valley. I thought of the column I wrote in *Popular Ceramics* and the thousands of friends it had helped me make. But all of this still did not add up.

"I've got an idea," I told Pappy later that evening. He peered over his paper quizzically: he has learned to be a little cautious when I announce a new brainstorm. "What now?" he asked.

"Let's quit ceramics."

"Let's!" he said, jumping up from his rocker. You've never seen a grin so broad.

The first problem was to get *out* of business. We had carloads of ceramics clay, mountains of tools, three thousand molds and shelf after shelf of greenware. We had a studio full of finished ceramic objects for sale. We had so much paraphernalia, in fact, that it took us almost a year to shake clear of ceramics. Not that we wanted to shake all the way out: we kept the studio as a small gift shop and every day someone drops in. We kept the workshop and the ladies of the valley are welcome to use it to make their own ceramics. We still have two kilns which are fired up from time to time. And I continue my "career" as mistress of ceremonies at various ceramics shows around the country.

It was easy enough to slough off the physical appurtenances of ceramics, but the memories of ten years or so of the wonderfully offbeat business stays with us.

I was writing my column for *Popular Ceramics* one day and, as usual, was rushed for time. The column always reminds me of the hundreds of people I have met through ceramics and, in a burst of inspiration, I wrote an invitation to my readers to come and see us on the river. "Come on the Fourth of July," I said. As insurance, I added a kicker: "Better bring some food along, in case we are swamped, and you'd better bring a sleeping bag, too." Actually, I did not take the invitation too seriously but it gave the column a nice ending and made me feel warm. After all, Scottsburg is twelve miles north of nowhere and surely not too many people would come. I expected a few Oregon ceramists and possibly one or two from northern California.

Pappy and I were away from home for a few days before the Fourth and only by dint of hard driving did we get back near midnight on the third. When we pulled off the highway, we found our yard full of cars and trailer coaches. "Looks like we've got company," I said. Pappy shook his head and grinned. "Sometimes I just can't keep up with you," he said. We went into the house. Luggage was strewn all over the floor and chairs. Pappy headed for his bed upstairs and popped right down again. "There are two women in my bed," he said. "You've got nothing on me," I countered. "There are two men in mine. I feel like the little bear in Goldilocks." We went to sleep in chairs.

At the crack of dawn I was awakened by a fantastic clattering of pots and pans in the kitchen. A great big handsome fellow, splendid in a blue robe complete with gold braid trim, was banging the pans around and whistling the Marine hymn. From time to time, he would unpucker his lips to let out full bodied song. "From the halls of Montezuma (bangbang) to the shores (bang) of Tripoli (bam) we will (bangbang) fight our country's ba-attles. . . ." He broke off his song and came over and nudged me. "Pardon me," he said, "but where do you think she keeps the coffee? Being a lady, I figured you could guess where a lady would hide it."

"Being a lady," I said, pretending to wake up, "I'd look in the cupboard behind the stove." A few minutes later he returned in an aura of coffee. He touched my shoulder again. "Lady, as a lady, you're a whiz," he grinned. "I found the coffee right where you said it would be. Like to have a cup?" I couldn't resist the aroma of steaming coffee right under my nose so I gave up my "sleep."

"You must have come in late," he said. "I've been so busy down by the river and hiking through the woods that I haven't even met the Workmans yet. Wait'll you get down to that river. It's about the prettiest thing I've

231

ever seen." He rambled on telling us about the wonders of our valley. I finally edged a word into his flow. "I'm Mrs. Workman," I said. His jaw dropped a bit. "Well, now," he said. "That's just fine." He must have been a little shocked, because he added, "You'll like it here."

"Are you interested in ceramics?"

"No," he laughed. "I was just driving by three nights ago and saw all the cars and your little sign, *Ceramics for Fun* and stopped to see what it was all about. Somebody said it would be all right for me to stay around for the Fourth of July. They said you wouldn't mind. I was lucky," he added, "I got the last bed."

Our guests have been a wonderful lot. They never seem to mind the crazy-house construction of our home (with almost every room on a slightly different level) or some inconveniences when we have a crowd. The serenity of the forest and the river, the frequent sight of otters playing tag and deer peering emotionally from the myrtle-wood, a taste of the simple life always seems to compensate for a lack of city conveniences. One of our friends, a buyer for a fashionable specialty store, loved to visit us but her nervous system began ringing bells after about three days of Umpqua: that was the limit of her metabolism for peace and quiet. She visited us first when we were still in the first shack. We thought she would be more comfortable across the highway in the Applegate's spare room, but she preferred our primitive quarters.

She soaked up the sun and the quiet for three days and then began to twitch. "I've had the country life for another year," she announced. "I'm all packed and ready to go." We urged her to stay but she demurred. "I've just got to get back to some excitement," she said, climbing into her car. At that moment, a speeding car missed the slight curve in front of our house, sailed gracefully down the slope and poked its nose through the shingles of the Applegate house, just between the twin beds of the spare bedroom, the one Maude and Paul had offered our guest. She stepped on the starter, gazed at the dust still settling around the wreckage of the Applegate manse, and rolled down the drive. "I better be getting back to Los Angeles," she said. "The excitement is quieter there." (Paul Applegate was resting on one of the beds. Imperturbable as ever, he raised himself on one elbow and addressed the driver. "Hello, neighbor," he said. "What brings you here?")

The nicest thing about our semi-retirement is that we can have more time with the people who visit us. Our original Fourth of July party has slipped its date a bit and now is an annual Labor Day party. With the help of our neighbors, who share their elk and venison and bear with us, we've had no trouble feeding our guests. What we can't provide, the guests themselves bring. This is an admirable arrangement because our guests include some great cooks. It is Pappy's firm belief that Hazel Dunmire of Portland makes the best huckleberry pie in Christendom—but he's had a long wait between pies.

Hazel and George Dunmire arrived at their first Labor Day festival with two pies and, long before Pappy got around to dessert, the pies had been devoured. The next year, aiming squarely at Pappy, Hazel brought three pies. Again Pappy missed out. The next year she arrived with nine pies, one especially dedicated to Pappy. She handed it to Val Martin. "Put this away so Pappy will be sure to get it," she said. As usual, Pappy was the last to eat and when he'd finished, he called for his special pie. Val Martin had already gone home and we could not find it. It was not in the freezer. It was not in the oven. It was not in the cupboards. "I guess I'm going through the rest of my life without ever tasting Hazel's huckleberry pie again," Pappy grumbled.

Shortly before Christmas, we had an unusual number of drop-ins, including my cousin, Lenore and her husband. They were assigned the unused lean-to which had been converted into a bedroom.

It was late when they arrived so Lenore very soon excused herself to go to bed and ducked into the lean-to. Almost immediately, she began broadcasting screams and we heard the sound of heavy blows being struck. We all rushed for the lean-to. Lenore was leaning weakly against the door frame, white with terror and liberally speckled with blood. "Over there," she wailed, pointing with a high-heeled shoe she held in her hand, also dripping blood. On a chair was a ghastly-looking object covered with fine, thick fur. It had been bashed into insensibility. But a closer look revealed the furry object was not and had never been animate. It was Hazel Dunmire's huckleberry pie. Three months in Oregon's moist climate, in the dark of the lean-to, had converted it into a lush dish of gray, furry mold. The blood was good, honest huckleberry juice.

We've had dozens of ceramists at our Labor Day parties, which we expected, but we have a lot of guests who wouldn't know ceramics from a hole in the ground, too. They have heard about the party and drop around for some human companionship and, perhaps, a helping of elk roast. We've had authors, photographers, at least one football coach, singers, salesmen and just plain people—and they've come from as far away as Hawaii and New York. One of my favorite guests, a "volunteer," comes every year to add to his collection of sunsets. "A sunset," he told us, "can make a man feel rich. I collect them wherever I can and then, on rainy nights, I take them all out and look at them again and again. Got them all in my mind. Beats a camera every time."

Not too long ago, I was to speak at the Grange and started with the usual, "Ladies and gentlemen . . ." but I felt a gentle tugging at my sleeve. It was Bertha Anderson who had introduced me. I leaned over to her and she whispered, "*Neighbors*, Gladys. You've forgotten we don't say 'ladies and gentlemen' at Grange. We always say '*neighbors.*'"

For a moment I was embarrassed by my oversight, and then decided to use it to make a special point about neighbors. I pretended I hadn't quite heard Bertha. "Ladies and gentlemen," I began again, "I am told it isn't proper to address you as ladies and gentlemen but I missed what Bertha said I *should* call you." I held my hand to my ear. Bertha whispered again: "*Neighbors.*"

"I don't get it," I said. "Please say it again."

At that point a boy in the front row held up his hand. "I know what you're supposed to call them," he said.

"You do? Fine; tell me—and say it real loud so everyone can hear," I invited.

235

Low Shoes, No Lipstick

"Sons o' bitches," shouted the precocious tyke. "That's what my Daddy calls 'em."

The hilarity that followed surprised the boy, and his father, I am sure, as well. I never heard what happened when they got home.

What the boy said was good for a laugh, but it was far, far from the truth. The mainest reason I know the boy's daddy was wrong is this: we've been in the valley for more than ten years now; we're no longer Drifters; this is our home. And I've seen love at work a hundred times for every time I've seen meanness or hate.

Occasionally some friend in one of the big cities asks me why we stay on the Umpqua. They are honestly puzzled about the values we find in this far-away corner of the United States. At first, I just replied, "We like it." More recently, I've come up with a better answer. "It's because of low shoes and no lipstick," I say.

And if this still leaves them puzzled, I can explain. Almost everywhere I've been, everyone seems to be trying to impress everyone else. On the Umpqua it's possible to be yourself. We wear house dresses. We wear low shoes—we even wear them with our formals at Grange ceremonies (and they're most practical in a country without sidewalks). We don't need beauty parlors or even lipstick to impress our neighbors. We arrive at meetings in jeeps, pickup trucks, jalopies and Cadillacs.

"Low shoes and no lipstick." It adds up to a valley of no pretensions. It adds up to absolute peace of mind. Almost.